REVELATION

THE GLORIFIED CHRIST

WOODROW KROLL

CROSSWAY BOOKS

A PUBLISHING MINISTRY OF
GOOD NEWS PUBLISHERS
WHEATON, ILLINOIS

Revelation: The Glorified Christ

Copyright © 2006 by Back to the Bible

Published by Crossway Books
      a publishing ministry of Good News Publishers
      1300 Crescent Street
      Wheaton, Illinois 60187

Cover design: Josh Dennis

Cover photo: iStock

First printing, 2006

Printed in the United States of America

ISBN 13: 978-1-58134-850-7
ISBN 10: 1-58134-850-9

Scripture quotations are taken from *The Holy Bible: English Standard Version*®. Copyright © 2001 by Crossway Bibles, a publishing ministry of Good News Publishers. Used by permission. All rights reserved.

Produced with the assistance of The Livingstone Corporation (www.LivingstoneCorp.com). Project staff: Neil Wilson

CH		16	15	14	13	12	11	10	09	08	07	06
15	14	13	12	11	10	9	8	7	6	5	4	3	2

Table of Contents

How to Use This Study

Your study of Revelation will have maximum impact if you prayerfully read each day's Scripture passage. The entire text of Revelation from the *The Holy Bible: English Standard Version* is printed before each day's reading, so that everything you need is in one place. While we recommend reading the Scripture passage before you read the devotional, some have found it helpful to use the devotional as preparation for reading the Scripture. If you are unfamiliar with the *English Standard Version* (on which this series of studies is based), you might consider reading the selection, then the devotional, followed by reading the passage again from a different Bible text with which you are more comfortable. This will give you an excellent basis for considering the rest of the lesson.

With each devotional there are three sections designed to help you better understand and apply the lesson's Scripture passage.

Go Deeper—The nature of this study makes it important to see Revelation in the context of other passages and insights from Scripture. This brief section will allow you to consider some of the implications of the day's passage for the central theme of the study (The Glorified Christ) as well as the way it fits with the rest of Scripture.

Express It—Suggestions for turning the insights from the lesson into prayer.

Consider It—Several questions will help you unpack and reflect on the Scripture passage of the day. These could be used for a small group discussion.

Introduction

Do you think of Revelation as a series of confusing images and puzzling events? It's true that no one may ever fully understand everything in this book, but this lesson will be well worth your time and help you form a more complete picture of Jesus.

Revelation 1:1–8

Prologue

1The revelation of Jesus Christ, which God gave him to show to his servants the things that must soon take place. He made it known by sending his angel to his servant John, ²who bore witness to the word of God and to the testimony of Jesus Christ, even to all that he saw. ³Blessed is the one who reads aloud the words of this prophecy, and blessed are those who hear, and who keep what is written in it, for the time is near.

Greeting to the Seven Churches

⁴John to the seven churches that are in Asia:

Grace to you and peace from him who is and who was and who is to come, and from the seven spirits who are before his throne, ⁵and from Jesus Christ the faithful witness, the firstborn of the dead, and the ruler of kings on earth.

To him who loves us and has freed us from our sins by his blood ⁶and made us a king-dom, priests to his God and Father, to him be glory and dominion forever and ever. Amen. ⁷Behold, he is coming with the clouds, and every eye will see him, even those who pierced him, and all tribes of the earth will wail on account of him. Even so. Amen.

⁸"I am the Alpha and the Omega," says the Lord God, "who is and who was and who is to come, the Almighty."

Key Verse

Blessed is the one who reads aloud the words of this prophecy, and blessed are those who hear, and who keep what is written in it, for the time is near (Rev. 1:3).

Go Deeper

These first eight verses already convey a panoramic picture of Jesus Christ. Jesus stretches our imagination to its limits. John includes numerous references to *who* Jesus is and *what* He does. Unfolding Jesus' char-acter, we can list among His titles: Christ (Rev.1–2, 5), "faithful witness" (v. 5), "first-born of the dead" (v. 5), "ruler of kings on earth" (v. 5), worthy of "glory and dominion forever" (v. 6).

(continued)

Go Deeper Continued

As God, Jesus also shares titles with God the Father: the source of "grace ... and peace" (v. 4), "who is and who was and who is to come" (vv. 4,8), "the Alpha and the Omega" (v. 8), and "the Almighty" (v. 8). For parallel passages, look at Daniel 7:13–14, Philippians 2:5–11, Colossians 1:15–19 and Hebrews 1:1–14.

P eople often fall into two very different groups when it comes to the Book of Revelation. The first group loves it. They speak its language. They listen to the news and read the papers each day, confident they can identify current events as partial or complete fulfillment of the grand events recorded in this last book of the Bible. They are ready to study Revelation at the drop of a hat. If you see yourself in that group, we pray you will find some fresh insight in these lessons.

The second group avoids Revelation like the plague. Frequently they admit their reaction isn't because they have tried to read the book themselves. They've just heard such negative comments that they've decided to skip the confusion. They have accepted Revelation's reputation as a book that can't be understood.

If you realize you're in that group, notice what today's key verse says—blessings are promised to those who read Revelation, not to those who understand it fully. And if you discover things in it "to keep" and you keep them, you will also be blessed. What better reason could we give you to undertake these lessons? God promises He will bless you if you read (or listen) to this part of His Word. Besides, you owe it to yourself and to the Lord to give Revelation a "firsthand" chance at you. You may be surprised at just how much you do understand!

As you begin, here are some helpful background notes. This book, like every book in the New Testament, has an assigned title. The original Scripture writers didn't give their books titles. The title for this last book in the Bible comes from the first line in the text: The Revelation of Jesus Christ. In casual conversation, it is typical to simply call the book "Revelation." Some people have the habit of referring to the book as "Revelations" (plural), but this is incorrect. God

As to what Jesus does, we find Him: being a faithful witness (v. 5), loving us (v. 5), freeing us from our sins (v. 5), making us a kingdom (v. 6), making us "priests to his God and Father" (v. 6). His past (and present) actions assure us of His future action, for "he is coming with the clouds" (v. 7). Keep these majestic glimpses in mind in the lessons to come as God fills in the picture for you by revealing anew His Son, Jesus Christ.

gave the apostle John *a* revelation of Jesus Christ. There may be many details, but there was only one revelation.

The word "of" in the phrase "revelation of Jesus Christ" can mean "about" or "belonging to." "Of" can refer to subject or possession. In this case, both uses fit. This amazing book reveals Jesus Christ in a way that belongs uniquely to Him. It came from Him and is ultimately about Him.

Think of Revelation more as a picture than a puzzle. If you expect to figure out the book completely, you will probably be disappointed. If you expect to meet the glorified Christ in His Revelation, you will be deeply satisfied. Keep asking the question, "What is Christ revealing about Himself in this passage?" This is true even when the passage doesn't mention Him directly. At first, you may have to settle for realizing that He is revealing that He knows what will happen. But, you may also be delighted to find that Jesus is revealing aspects of His character and majesty in new ways. Consider this part of your blessing.

You may be aware that Revelation gets read and interpreted in several different ways. Briefly, these approaches boil down to one prophetic approach and a group of non-prophetic approaches. All the approaches agree on some facts: Revelation was written in the past, part of Revelation concerns the past (especially the first three chapters) and certain events in Revelation parallel experiences that Christians have had over the centuries.

At this point, the non-prophetic groups have several ways of stating that Revelation as a whole is about the past. They believe it does not describe specific future events (with the possible exception of the Second Coming of Christ). Basically, these approaches turn Revelation into a book of history with little to say to us today.

> *" Think of Revelation more as a picture than a puzzle. If you expect to figure out the book completely, you will probably be disappointed. If you expect to meet the glorified Christ in His Revelation, you will be deeply satisfied. "*

The prophetic group maintains that despite parallels and similarities throughout history, Revelation contains a vivid picture of *final* events in world history. Please note these lessons are written with this prophetic perspective in mind—and for good reasons.

In the opening verses, John calls what he is sending the churches "this prophecy" (v. 3). As we will see in the next lesson, Jesus Himself described the contents of this book in a way that directs us to consider it prophetically. God provided the Revelation of Jesus Christ as much for us as for the first century believers. It can speak to us as powerfully as it spoke to them. What they needed to see in Revelation is the same awesome picture we need to see—the glorified Christ!

Express It

As you pray about this study, ask God to help you set aside any negative or preconceived attitude about Revelation so you can experience the book on its own terms. Give the Holy Spirit permission to keep reminding you to ask, "How is this passage revealing Jesus Christ to me?"

Consider It

As you read Revelation 1:1–8, consider these questions:

1) Why do you want to study Revelation?

2) When God promises to bless you, what do you expect will happen?

3) How do these first verses reveal Jesus Christ to you in both new ways and familiar ways?

4) Where's the good news for you in these verses?

5) What do you know about the apostle John?

6) How does it affect you when you read that God offers "grace" and "peace" to you (v. 4)?

7) What's your attitude about the possibility that Jesus could return today?

Face-to-Face with Christ

Do you know how you would respond if Jesus showed up today? It would probably be very similar to the apostle John's response. As you get face-to-face with Jesus in this lesson, you'll see Him in all His glory. You'll also be reminded you have been called to be a "light to the world."

Revelation 1:9–20

Vision of the Son of Man

⁹I, John, your brother and partner in the tribulation and the kingdom and the patient endurance that are in Jesus, was on the island called Patmos on account of the word of God and the testimony of Jesus. ¹⁰I was in the Spirit on the Lord's day, and I heard behind me a loud voice like a trumpet ¹¹saying, "Write what you see in a book and send it to the seven churches, to Ephesus and to Smyrna and to Pergamum and to Thyatira and to Sardis and to Philadelphia and to Laodicea."

¹²Then I turned to see the voice that was speaking to me, and on turning I saw seven golden lampstands, ¹³and in the midst of the lampstands one like a son of man, clothed with a long robe and with a golden sash around his chest. ¹⁴The hairs of his head were white like wool, as white as snow. His eyes were like a flame of fire, ¹⁵his feet were like burnished bronze, refined in a furnace, and his voice was like the roar of many waters. ¹⁶In his right hand he held seven stars, from his mouth came a sharp two-edged sword, and his face was like the sun shining in full strength.

¹⁷When I saw him, I fell at his feet as though dead. But he laid his right hand on me, saying, "Fear not, I am the first and the last, ¹⁸and the living one. I died, and behold I am alive forevermore, and I have the keys of Death and Hades. ¹⁹Write therefore the things that you have seen, those that are and those that are to take place after this. ²⁰As for the mystery of the seven stars that you saw in my right hand, and the seven golden lampstands, the seven stars are the angels of the seven churches, and the seven lampstands are the seven churches.

Key Verse

"Write therefore the things that you have seen, those that are and those that are to take place after this" (Rev. 1:19).

Go Deeper

This was not the first time John saw Jesus in a glorified state. Matthew 17:1–13, Mark 9:2–13 and Luke 9:28–36 give us three versions of the Transfiguration, when the Lord joined Moses and Elijah, taking on a remarkable appearance.

And yet as powerful as Christ's glorified appearance may be, John was taken with the

(continued)

way Jesus revealed His inner glory, His uniqueness, even when He walked among men. In the beginning of his Gospel, John declares, "And the Word became flesh and dwelt among us, and we have seen his glory, glory as of the only Son from the Father, full of grace and truth" (John 1:14).

Much earlier, the prophet Daniel saw a

The aging apostle John got a surprise visitor—Jesus. Decades after the Lord ascended to heaven outside Jerusalem, the glorified Christ unexpectedly appeared behind His last living apostle on the Lord's Day.

At first, John just heard a loud voice giving him an assignment. He was told to record what he saw "in a book and send it to the seven churches" (Rev. 1:11). Although there was a special message for each of the churches, John would write one book for seven churches—not seven letters to seven churches. Each of the churches would have access to what Jesus said about all of them. Jesus had a message for His Church, and He wanted it recorded in an open book for the ages.

John turned around and found himself in an ultimate show-and-tell experience. He saw seven golden lampstands and one shining figure. John's description of the "one like a son of man" (v. 13) takes several sentences, but his reaction to the figure took a mere instant. When John saw the glorified Christ, he dropped like a stone.

Take a moment to re-read verses 12–16. Notice how the description seems to grow in intensity. There's nothing that odd about a long robe and a golden sash. The brilliant white wool-like hair jolts our typical mental picture of Jesus. The flaming eyes are difficult to look at, but when we lower ours, the reflection off the bronzed feet is almost blinding. The voice like a waterfall draws our attention, and we are stunned to see a razor-like, double-edged sword coming from His mouth.

Now stop, close your eyes and imagine hearing an indescribable voice behind you say, "I'm here." Don't turn; just take in the moment. Can you begin to identify with the way John was overwhelmed in meeting Christ face-to-face?

vision of someone whose "clothing was white as snow, and the hair of his head like pure wool" (Dan. 7:9). In Philippians 2:7, Paul tells us that Jesus "made himself nothing, taking the form of a servant, being born in the likeness of men." The glory that Jesus set aside when He came to us as man He reclaimed after His Resurrection and ascension. John came face-to-face with the glorified Christ!

An encounter with the glorified Christ is never a casual experience. Steven saw the glorified Christ and forgot about the stones raining down on him (Acts 7). Paul met Jesus and got knocked to the ground (Acts 9). Even an angelic messenger who reflects Christ's glory evokes terror and awe in us. Those contacts always involve the words, "Fear not." But before he heard these words, John felt the hand of Jesus reach down and touch him. Jesus overwhelms and affirms in the same moment. Jesus isn't someone you know casually.

The specific assignment Jesus gave John provides the guidelines for this study. It determines how we will approach Revelation together. We will read "the things that you [John] have seen, those that are and those that are to take place after this" (Rev. 1:19).

The first phrase, "the things that you have seen," refers to John's immediate experience. He recorded the setting and the first startling parts of Christ's revelation to him. The phrase "things that are" refers to the present circumstances, which Jesus is about to describe. These "things that are" have to do with the condition of Jesus' Church, represented in various cities. They have to do with the ongoing challenges that confront the Church of Jesus Christ and the consequences that follow when faithfulness falters. These are the things that *always* are, for they describe the opposition faced by the Church throughout the centuries (Rev. 2–3).

The phrase, "those that are to take place after this," refers to what Jesus will show John regarding events beyond the Church age. This last phrase is prophetic language. It states that John will write about things not yet seen and which are not yet. What begins in chapter 4 is a vision of the future—future for John and his time and future for us as well.

In Jesus' first words to John, He listed the seven churches He intended to be included in His "state of the Church" message. If you

> " *A disconnected chandelier is about as useful as a flameless lampstand. It may be nice to look at, but it isn't accomplishing its purpose—to give light.* "

have a map in your Bible, you can locate these churches in the western part of present-day Turkey. Beginning with Ephesus, the cities listed form a rough circle, listed clockwise.

Jesus explains that the seven lampstands surrounding Him represent the seven churches He has chosen to review. Why lampstands? If the passage said "chandeliers," you would immediately connect the object with its purpose—to give light. Lampstands in John's day are like chandeliers today. One of Jesus' original challenges to His followers was, "You are the light of the world ... let your light shine before others, so that they may see your good works and give glory to your Father who is in heaven" (Matt. 5:14,16).

A disconnected chandelier is about as useful as a flameless lampstand. It may be nice to look at, but it isn't accomplishing its purpose—to give light. This is almost exactly the point that Jesus makes about the seven churches. He finds items to commend in them, but five out of the seven also receive a sober warning from their Master. We need to hear and heed that warning.

Express It

Every time you pause to pray, you are in exactly the same place John occupied on that Sunday morning long ago. Christ is present. You may not see His glorified state, but you have the assurance of His presence. In the context of this prophetic study, pray with Jesus' comforting words in mind: "I am with you always, to the end of the age" (Matt. 28:20).

Consider It

As you read Revelation 1:9–20, consider these questions:

1) How would your worship attitude be next Sunday if you expected Jesus to show up for a visit with you?

2) In what ways does isolation (like John's isolation on the island of Patmos) sharpen or dull your awareness of God?

3) How would you describe the present assignment in life you have received from God?

4) What stands out the most for you about John's description of Christ? Why?

5) When Jesus says He has the "keys of Death and Hades" (v. 18), what does that mean?

6) In what ways are you involved and committed to the quality of "light" that your local church shines in the world?

7) How are you affected by Jesus' touch and His assurance that you should "fear not"?

Lesson

3

The Message to the Seven Churches

Jesus has called us to be "conquerors," but what are we fighting against? This passage looks at the letters John sent to seven select churches. By looking at where Jesus commends and rebukes them, we can see the enemies we face today—and how to confront them.

Revelation 2:1–3:22

To the Church in Ephesus

2"To the angel of the church in Ephesus write: 'The words of him who holds the seven stars in his right hand, who walks among the seven golden lampstands.

²"'I know your works, your toil and your patient endurance, and how you cannot bear with those who are evil, but have tested those who call themselves apostles and are not, and found them to be false. ³I know you are enduring patiently and bearing up for my name's sake, and you have not grown weary. ⁴But I have this against you, that you have abandoned the love you had at first. ⁵Remember therefore from where you have fallen; repent, and do the works you did at first. If not, I will come to you and remove your lampstand from its place, unless you repent. ⁶Yet this you have: you hate the works of the Nicolaitans, which I also hate. ⁷He who has an ear, let him hear what the Spirit says to the churches. To the one who conquers I will grant to eat of the tree of life, which is in the paradise of God.'

To the Church in Smyrna

⁸"And to the angel of the church in Smyrna write: 'The words of the first and the last, who died and came to life.

⁹"'I know your tribulation and your poverty (but you are rich) and the slander of those who say that they are Jews and are not, but are a synagogue of Satan. ¹⁰Do not fear what you are about to suffer. Behold, the devil is about to throw some of you into prison, that you may be tested, and for ten days you will have tribulation. Be faithful unto death, and I will give you the crown of life. ¹¹He who has an ear, let him hear what the Spirit says to the churches. The one who conquers will not be hurt by the second death.'

To the Church in Pergamum

¹²"And to the angel of the church in Pergamum write: 'The words of him who has the sharp two-edged sword.

¹³"'I know where you dwell, where Satan's throne is. Yet you hold fast my name, and you did not deny my faith even in the days of Antipas my faithful witness, who was killed among you, where Satan dwells. ¹⁴But I have a few things against you: you have some there who hold the teaching of Balaam, who taught Balak to put a stumbling block before the sons of Israel, so that they might eat food sacrificed to idols and practice sexual immorality. ¹⁵So also you have some who hold the teaching of the Nicolaitans. ¹⁶Therefore repent. If not, I will come to you soon and war against them with the sword of my mouth. ¹⁷He who has an ear, let him hear what the Spirit says to the churches. To the one who conquers I will give some of the hidden manna, and I will give him a white stone, with a new name written on the stone that no one knows except the one who receives it.'

To the Church in Thyatira

[18]"And to the angel of the church in Thyatira write: 'The words of the Son of God, who has eyes like a flame of fire, and whose feet are like burnished bronze.

[19]"'I know your works, your love and faith and service and patient endurance, and that your latter works exceed the first. [20]But I have this against you, that you tolerate that woman Jezebel, who calls herself a prophetess and is teaching and seducing my servants to practice sexual immorality and to eat food sacrificed to idols. [21]I gave her time to repent, but she refuses to repent of her sexual immorality. [22]Behold, I will throw her onto a sickbed, and those who commit adultery with her I will throw into great tribulation, unless they repent of her works, [23]and I will strike her children dead. And all the churches will know that I am he who searches mind and heart, and I will give to each of you as your works deserve. [24]But to the rest of you in Thyatira, who do not hold this teaching, who have not learned what some call the deep things of Satan, to you I say, I do not lay on you any other burden. [25]Only hold fast what you have until I come. [26]The one who conquers and who keeps my works until the end, to him I will give authority over the nations, [27]and he will rule them with a rod of iron, as when earthen pots are broken in pieces, even as I myself have received authority from my Father. [28]And I will give him the morning star. [29]He who has an ear, let him hear what the Spirit says to the churches.'

To the Church in Sardis

3"And to the angel of the church in Sardis write: 'The words of him who has the seven spirits of God and the seven stars.

"'I know your works. You have the reputation of being alive, but you are dead. [2]Wake up, and strengthen what remains and is about to die, for I have not found your works complete in the sight of my God. [3]Remember, then, what you received and heard. Keep it, and repent. If you will not wake up, I will come like a thief, and you will not know at what hour I will come against you. [4]Yet you have still a few names in Sardis, people who have not soiled their garments, and they will walk with me in white, for they are worthy. [5]The one who conquers will be clothed thus in white garments, and I will never blot his name out of the book of life. I will confess his name before my Father and before his angels. [6]He who has an ear, let him hear what the Spirit says to the churches.'

To the Church in Philadelphia

[7]"And to the angel of the church in Philadelphia write: 'The words of the holy one, the true one, who has the key of David, who opens and no one will shut, who shuts and no one opens.

[8]"'I know your works. Behold, I have set before you an open door, which no one is able to shut. I know that you have but little power, and yet you have kept my word and have not denied my name. [9]Behold, I will make those of the synagogue of Satan who say that they are Jews and are not, but lie— behold, I will make them come and bow

down before your feet and they will learn that I have loved you. ¹⁰Because you have kept my word about patient endurance, I will keep you from the hour of trial that is coming on the whole world, to try those who dwell on the earth. ¹¹I am coming soon. Hold fast what you have, so that no one may seize your crown. ¹²The one who conquers, I will make him a pillar in the temple of my God. Never shall he go out of it, and I will write on him the name of my God, and the name of the city of my God, the new Jerusalem, which comes down from my God out of heaven, and my own new name. ¹³He who has an ear, let him hear what the Spirit says to the churches.'

To the Church in Laodicea

¹⁴"And to the angel of the church in Laodicea write: 'The words of the Amen, the faithful and true witness, the beginning of God's creation.

¹⁵"'I know your works: you are neither cold nor hot. Would that you were either cold or hot! ¹⁶So, because you are lukewarm, and neither hot nor cold, I will spit you out of my mouth. ¹⁷For you say, I am rich, I have prospered, and I need nothing, not realizing that you are wretched, pitiable, poor, blind, and naked. ¹⁸I counsel you to buy from me gold refined by fire, so that you may be rich, and white garments so that you may clothe yourself and the shame of your nakedness may not be seen, and salve to anoint your eyes, so that you may see. ¹⁹Those whom I love, I reprove and discipline, so be zealous and repent. ²⁰Behold, I stand at the door and knock. If anyone hears my voice and opens

> # Key Verse
>
> *"'The one who conquers, I will grant him to sit with me on my throne, as I also conquered and sat down with my Father on his throne'"* (Rev. 3:21).

the door, I will come in to him and eat with him, and he with me. ²¹The one who conquers, I will grant him to sit with me on my throne, as I also conquered and sat down with my Father on his throne. ²²He who has an ear, let him hear what the Spirit says to the churches.'"

Go Deeper

When we read Jesus' repeated challenges to be people who "conquer," our first response may be fear or terror. Perhaps we feel like we've already lost. Or we may feel like our lives represent at least as much losing as they do overcoming and conquering.

But we can have hope. This word "conquer" is included in one of the greatest pas-

(continued)

sages about confidence and hope in all the Bible. Let your soul rest in the following words: "No, in all these things we are *more than conquerors* through him who loved us. For I am sure that neither death nor life, nor angels nor rulers, nor things present nor

Jesus instructed John to write memos to seven churches. The Lord had individual comments for each church. But did He have a central message for all of them? Do these memos share a common theme?

Yes, they do. Yet each of these churches was unique in setting and condition. The challenges they faced and the concerns Jesus expressed, however, certainly still echo in churches today. Any church at any time can find both encouragement and warning in these memos from Jesus. Some have even traced the development of the Church through the ages using these seven churches in Revelation. They were certainly not chosen at random. But before we look at that central and lasting message, let's look briefly at how these churches differed.

The church in Ephesus (Rev. 2:1–7) was a successful megachurch. It was the apostle John's home church. His reputation probably drew many seekers. Jesus commended them for their excellent labors but also confronted them because they had "abandoned the love you had at first" (v. 4).

The church in Smyrna (2:8–11) lived as a persecuted church. There would be more suffering in their future but a promise of the crown of life. Their review by Jesus is entirely positive.

Jesus described the church in Pergamum (2:12–17) as His church in a bad neighborhood. He affirmed their faithfulness but warned against their acceptance of evil teachers. They were in danger of compromising their faith. Jesus called them to repentance.

When Jesus described the church in Thyatira (2:18–29), He noted not only admirable qualities but also an increase in acts of service. But He confronted their reputation as "The Universal Church of things to come, nor powers, nor height nor depth, nor anything else in all creation, will be able to separate us from the love of God in Christ Jesus our Lord" (Rom. 8:37–39, emphasis added).

Jesus will not ask you to do what He will not help you to do. You can trust Him to make you into one who conquers.

Toleration." They were allowing a "Jezebel" to teach immorality among them. Jesus insisted that her followers must repent, and He comforted those who had resisted the temptation of Satan.

Jesus described the church in Sardis (3:1–6) as little more than a morgue with a steeple. They appeared alive (and some believers in the church were definitely alive), but when Jesus looked, He saw lethargy and deadness. They needed to wake up!

Jesus commended Philadelphia's church (3:7–13) as the faithful "Chapel of Opportunity." He saw they were obedient within their limitations. He promised them "an open door" (v. 8) of effectiveness and His personal protection in difficult times ahead.

Jesus described the church in Laodicea (3:14–22) as the big downtown church facing subtle temptations in the heart of the city. They blended more and more into the downtown scene rather than standing apart as a witness for Christ. Their lukewarmness made them distasteful to Jesus. He challenged them to move one way or the other rather than wallow in the middle without a clear purpose.

These cities represent seven places where the Gospel had taken root. Jesus cared deeply for each one. They were all local expressions of His Body. He acknowledged their uniqueness. Yet to every one He also issued the same warning and promise: "Listen, and I will reward those who conquer." (See 2:7, 11, 17, 26–29 and 3:5–6, 12–13, 21–22.) This lesson's key verse highlights one of these promises: "The one who conquers, I will grant him to sit with me on my throne, as I also conquered and sat down with my Father on his throne" (3:21).

Whether we apply an approach that sees the seven churches as a general cross-section of church challenges, or we see a prophetic outline of the stages in church history in these chapters, neither the warnings nor the promises change. They apply to individuals as well as churches at any moment. They apply to us, now.

> *Even though events around us may demand our attention, and our own fears and feelings may try to distract us, we must keep listening to what the Holy Spirit says to us in His inspired Word.*

Jesus tells us we must diligently listen to what the Holy Spirit says. Even though events around us may demand our attention, and our own fears and feelings may try to distract us, we must keep listening to what the Holy Spirit says to us in His inspired Word. And we must be attentive to the Spirit bearing witness with our spirits that we are God's children. (See Rom. 8:16.) Only then can we hope to "conquer."

It is by God's Spirit that we persevere, overcome and conquer. These victorious words will stiffen our resolve as long as we keep Jesus' experience in mind. The key verse reminds us that He "conquered," but we know what that involved: suffering, disappointment, hardship and death. We hope to conquer, not because it will be easy, but because Jesus Himself is in us to make victory possible. We can look forward with joy to Jesus' promise: "I will grant him to sit with me on my throne" (Rev. 3:21). Where else would we want to spend eternity?

Express It

As you pray today, lift up the leadership of the church in which you are a member. Pray that God's Spirit will help them model a life of listening to Him and a life of conquering. Ask God for wisdom in identifying and fulfilling the role He has for you within the church. Express as clearly as you can your understanding of what it means to depend fully on Him for guidance and strength in order to conquer.

Consider It

As you read Revelation 2:1–3:22, consider these questions:

1) How many of these church challenges and weaknesses have you observed in action?

_____

_____

_____

2) Which church in Revelation shares the most characteristics with your local church?

_____

_____

3) How do you think Jesus would commend and challenge your church if it was added to the list in Revelation?

_____

_____

_____

4) In what senses would you say that the church in Laodicea seems to represent the general state of the Christian church in the world today?

_____

_____

_____

5) How do you understand Jesus' challenge to "hear what the Spirit says to the churches" in your daily life?

_____

_____

_____

6) In what ways would you say you are making progress in being one who conquers as Jesus describes it in these chapters?

_____

_____

_____

7) What are you looking forward to about sitting with Christ?

_____

_____

_____

Lesson

4

God's Throne Room

The stage is now set for the rest of Revelation. And what a stage it is—the very throne room of heaven! In this lesson, you'll see evidence of God's holiness, His greatness and His worthiness of passing judgment and receiving honor. And you'll be invited to join a choir as they sing praises to the Most High God.

Revelation 4:1–5:14

The Throne in Heaven

4After this I looked, and behold, a door standing open in heaven! And the first voice, which I had heard speaking to me like a trumpet, said, "Come up here, and I will show you what must take place after this." ²At once I was in the Spirit, and behold, a throne stood in heaven, with one seated on the throne. ³And he who sat there had the appearance of jasper and carnelian, and around the throne was a rainbow that had the appearance of an emerald. ⁴Around the throne were twenty-four thrones, and seated on the thrones were twenty-four elders, clothed in white garments, with golden crowns on their heads. ⁵From the throne came flashes of lightning, and rumblings and peals of thunder, and before the throne were burning seven torches of fire, which are the seven spirits of God, and before the throne there was as it were a sea of glass, like crystal.

And around the throne, on each side of the throne, are four living creatures, full of eyes in front and behind: ⁷the first living creature like a lion, the second living creature like an ox, the third living creature with the face of a man, and the fourth living creature like an eagle in flight. ⁸And the four living creatures, each of them with six wings, are full of eyes all around and within, and day and night they never cease to say,

"Holy, holy, holy, is the Lord God Almighty,

who was and is and is to come!"

⁹And whenever the living creatures give glory and honor and thanks to him who is seated on the throne, who lives forever and ever, ¹⁰the twenty-four elders fall down before him who is seated on the throne and worship him who lives forever and ever. They cast their crowns before the throne, saying,

¹¹"Worthy are you, our Lord and God,

to receive glory and honor and power,

for you created all things,

and by your will they existed and
were created."

Key Verse

At once I was in the Spirit, and behold, a throne stood in heaven, with one seated on the throne (Rev. 4:2).

The Scroll and the Lamb

5Then I saw in the right hand of him who was seated on the throne a scroll written within and on the back, sealed with seven seals. ²And I saw a strong angel proclaiming with a loud voice, "Who is worthy to open the scroll and break its seals?" ³And no one in heaven or on earth or under the earth was able to open the scroll or to look into it, ⁴and I began to weep loudly because no one was found worthy to open the scroll or to look into it. ⁵And one of the elders said to me, "Weep no more; behold, the Lion of the tribe of Judah, the Root of David, has conquered, so that he can open the scroll and its seven seals."

⁶And between the throne and the four living creatures and among the elders I saw a Lamb standing, as though it had been slain, with seven horns and with seven eyes, which are the seven spirits of God sent out into all the earth. ⁷And he went and took the scroll from the right hand of him who was seated on the throne. ⁸And when he had taken the scroll, the four living creatures and the twenty-four elders fell down before the Lamb, each holding a harp, and golden bowls full of incense, which are the prayers of the saints. ⁹And they sang a new song, saying,

"Worthy are you to take the scroll
and to open its seals,

for you were slain, and by your blood
you ransomed people for God
from every tribe and language and
people and nation,

¹⁰and you have made them a kingdom
and priests to our God,
and they shall reign on the earth."

¹¹Then I looked, and I heard around the throne and the living creatures and the elders the voice of many angels, numbering myriads of myriads and thousands of thousands, ¹²saying with a loud voice, "Worthy is the Lamb who was slain, to receive power and wealth and wisdom and might and honor and glory and blessing!" ¹³And I heard every creature in heaven and on earth and under the earth and in the sea, and all that is in them, saying, "To him who sits on the throne and to the Lamb be blessing and honor and glory and might forever and ever!" ¹⁴And the four living creatures said, "Amen!" and the elders fell down and worshiped.

Go Deeper

With the first verse of chapter 5 a tense drama begins to unfold in God's throne room. John sees a great scroll covered with writing but firmly sealed. When John hears the angel ask, "Who is worthy to open the scroll and break its seals?" (v. 2), the question seems to cast such doubt on the task that John begins to weep in despair. But he's basically told by an elder, "John, stop crying. That was a rhetorical question. We all know there is One, the conquering Lion of Judah, who

(continued

can break the seals and open the scroll."

John may have expected to see the impressive Lion of Judah when he looked near the throne, but instead he saw the Lamb of God. This surprise reminds us of a mistake we frequently make when we think about God. We try to "domesticate Him." We want the Lion of Judah to be cuddly and tame like a lamb. Instead we meet the Lamb of God who roars like a lion! This is the glorified Christ. He truly is worthy of our worship, our obedience and our very lives.

I n the first three chapters of Revelation, Jesus came to John. Beginning with chapter 4, the Lord took John on a heart-stopping, eye-popping tour of the future. As was the case in 1:10, John was again "in the Spirit" for these moments. He was immediately told what to expect in this encounter: "Come up here, and I will show you what must take place after this" (Rev. 4:1). John was about to witness events to come.

Among the changes that occur right here in the Book of Revelation, one deserves immediate mention. During the first three chapters, the word "church" is used 19 times. The Church is not mentioned again until Revelation 22:16, when John was reminded why he was given this amazing vision.

How do we explain the sudden silence about the Church in the 18 chapters that describe the horrific judgment of God on the earth? The most obvious explanation is that the Church isn't mentioned because it isn't *here*. Followers of Christ have been suddenly removed from the earthly scene by an act of God frequently called the Rapture of the church.

This event is most clearly described in 1 Thessalonians 4:13–18, a passage that has striking similarities with the first verses of chapter 4 of Revelation. To the Thessalonians, the apostle Paul wrote, "But we do not want you to be uninformed, brothers, about those who are asleep, that you may not grieve as others do who have no hope. For since we believe that Jesus died and rose again, even so, through Jesus, God will bring with him those who have fallen asleep. For this we declare to you by a word from the Lord, that we who are alive, who are left until the coming of the Lord, will not precede those who have fallen asleep. For the Lord himself will descend from heav-

> **"** *How willing are we to enter into the wholehearted praise for God the Almighty that constantly fills the throne room of God?* **"**

en with a cry of command, with the voice of an archangel, and with the sound of the trumpet of God. And the dead in Christ will rise first. Then we who are alive, who are left, will be caught up together with them in the clouds to meet the Lord in the air, and so we will always be with the Lord. Therefore encourage one another with these words" (1 Thess. 4:13–18).

Note how verse 16 parallels the details John included in Revelation 4:1: the voice, the trumpet and the command. Apparently the order to "Come up here" must have sounded like the order Jesus gave outside the grave of Lazarus. On that occasion, the Lord specified the command by saying, "Lazarus, come out" (John 11:43). Had He simply shouted, "Come out" who knows how many dead people would have leaped from their tombs! The radical change of participants in the following chapters of Revelation can best be explained by assuming the church is removed before the "tribulations" that will come upon earth.

At that point, the raptured Church will see what John saw in his vision—the throne of God. The scene he described conveys awesome holiness prepared to pass judgment. As we would expect, John couldn't describe God (see John 1:18), only His appearance. "God is light" (1 John 1:5), but what struck John was a combination of colors, not simply bright, blinding light. The colors, which John compared with jewels, represent aspects of God's character. The jasper stone (Rev. 21:11) is a crystal-clear white mineral highlighting God's purity and glory. Carnelian jewels have a ruby-red, blood-like color, reminding us of God's redemptive nature—His willingness to save the lost. Around all of this, the apostle saw a rainbow wreath. He couldn't quite see the throne itself because there were constant flashes of lightning and rumbles of thunder. The divine court was in session.

John next describes the actors in the scene, a mix of humans, angels and creatures. The 24 elders aren't specifically identified, but it makes sense to see them as representatives of the Church. They are seated on thrones of their own. The first four creatures (lion-like, ox-like, man-like and eagle-like) all have wings and multiple eyes. They surround God's throne. They continually repeat a phrase of praise to the Lord God Almighty (4:8). Meanwhile, the elders respond by bowing before God's throne, proclaiming God's worthiness and offering their crowns of faithfulness as gestures of worship (vv. 9–11).

All of these observations prepare us for the apparent crisis John witnesses next. He sees a huge scroll, covered in writing, but firmly sealed. And he notices a Lamb standing right beside God's throne. All of the necessary actors in the drama that will now unfold are on the scene. In the next few moments, John will cease to be an awestruck observer and become a participant. But let's first pause and take in the glory of God ourselves. How willing are we to enter into the wholehearted praise for God the Almighty that constantly fills the throne room of God?

Express It

As you pray, sit quietly for a few minutes and ponder what John is describing when he talks about being "in the Spirit." Request that God fill you with an awareness of His presence, person, and power. Ask Him to train you to be open to Him in the same way that John reports. Don't be too concerned about what you might feel, but simply acknowledge God's presence in your life. Thank Him for what He has allowed you to "see" about Him in these chapters of Revelation.

Consider It

As you read Revelation 4:1–5:14, consider these questions:

1) What do you find most difficult to imagine about God's throne room?

2) What part of the scene in chapter 4 makes you curious or excited about entering heaven?

3) How would you explain the statement of praise made by the four creatures around the throne (4:8)? What do they mean by "Holy, holy, holy"?

4) Why do you think the 24 elders respond to the words of the creatures the way they do (4:9–11)?

5) How does the response of the elders (4:11) compare with the praise of the creatures?

6) What does it mean for God to receive glory and honor and power? Aren't these things He has already? How could you "give" them to Him?

7) Who is the Lamb described in chapter 5? If you only had these two chapters to go by, what could you say about the importance of the Lamb?

8) What difference does the message of these two chapters make in your life?

Lesson
5

Cracking the Seals

As the beginning of the end approaches, we see Jesus bringing justice to the earth. But even as He punishes the wicked for their sins, He still brings salvation to those who honestly seek Him. As you go through this lesson, you'll see how important it is to make that decision while you can.

Revelation 6:1–7:17

The Seven Seals

6Now I watched when the Lamb opened one of the seven seals, and I heard one of the four living creatures say with a voice like thunder, "Come!" ²And I looked, and behold, a white horse! And its rider had a bow, and a crown was given to him, and he came out conquering, and to conquer.

³When he opened the second seal, I heard the second living creature say, "Come!" ⁴And out came another horse, bright red. Its rider was permitted to take peace from the earth, so that men should slay one another, and he was given a great sword.

⁵When he opened the third seal, I heard the third living creature say, "Come!" And I looked, and behold, a black horse! And its rider had a pair of scales in his hand. ⁶And I heard what seemed to be a voice in the midst of the four living creatures, saying, "A quart of wheat for a denarius, and three quarts of barley for a denarius, and do not harm the oil and wine!"

⁷When he opened the fourth seal, I heard the voice of the fourth living creature say, "Come!" ⁸And I looked, and behold, a pale horse! And its rider's name was Death, and Hades followed him. And they were given authority over a fourth of the earth, to kill with sword and with famine and with pestilence and by wild beasts of the earth.

⁹When he opened the fifth seal, I saw under the altar the souls of those who had been slain for the word of God and for the witness they had borne. ¹⁰They cried out with a loud voice, "O Sovereign Lord, holy and true, how long before you will judge and avenge our blood on those who dwell on the earth?" ¹¹Then they were each given a white robe and told to rest a little longer, until the number of their fellow servants and their brothers should be complete, who were to be killed as they themselves had been.

¹²When he opened the sixth seal, I looked, and behold, there was a great earthquake, and the sun became black as sackcloth, the full moon became like blood, ¹³and the stars of the sky fell to the earth as the fig tree sheds its winter fruit when shaken by a gale. ¹⁴The sky vanished like a scroll that is being rolled up, and every mountain and island was removed from its place. ¹⁵Then the kings of the earth and the great ones and the generals and the rich and the powerful, and everyone, slave and free, hid themselves in the caves and among the rocks of the mountains, ¹⁶calling to the mountains and rocks, "Fall on us and hide us from the face of him who is seated on the throne, and from the wrath of the Lamb, ¹⁷for the great day of their wrath has come, and who can stand?"

The 144,000 of Israel Sealed

7After this I saw four angels standing at the four corners of the earth, holding back the four winds of the earth, that no wind might blow on earth or sea or against any tree. ²Then I saw another angel ascending from the rising of the sun, with the seal of the living God, and he called with a loud voice to the four angels who had been given power to harm earth and sea, ³saying, "Do not harm the earth or the sea or the trees, until we have sealed the servants of our God on their foreheads." ⁴And I heard the number of the sealed, 144,000, sealed from every tribe of the sons of Israel:

⁵12,000 from the tribe of Judah were sealed,

12,000 from the tribe of Reuben,

12,000 from the tribe of Gad,

⁶12,000 from the tribe of Asher,

12,000 from the tribe of Naphtali,

12,000 from the tribe of Manasseh,

⁷12,000 from the tribe of Simeon,

12,000 from the tribe of Levi,

12,000 from the tribe of Issachar,

⁸12,000 from the tribe of Zebulun,

12,000 from the tribe of Joseph,

12,000 from the tribe of Benjamin were sealed.

A Great Multitude from Every Nation

⁹After this I looked, and behold, a great multitude that no one could number, from every nation, from all tribes and peoples and languages, standing before the throne and before the Lamb, clothed in white robes, with palm branches in their hands, ¹⁰and crying out with a loud voice, "Salvation belongs to our God who sits on the throne, and to the Lamb!" ¹¹And all the angels were standing around the throne and around the elders and the four living creatures, and they fell on their faces before the throne and worshiped

> # Key Verse
>
> *Now I watched when the Lamb opened one of the seven seals, and I heard one of the four living creatures say with a voice like thunder, "Come!"* (Rev. 6:1).

God, ¹²saying, "Amen! Blessing and glory and wisdom and thanksgiving and honor and power and might be to our God forever and ever! Amen."

¹³Then one of the elders addressed me, saying, "Who are these, clothed in white robes, and from where have they come?" ¹⁴I said to him, "Sir, you know." And he said to me, "These are the ones coming out of the great tribulation. They have washed their robes and made them white in the blood of the Lamb.

¹⁵"Therefore they are before the throne of God,

and serve him day and night in his temple;

and he who sits on the throne will shelter them with his presence.

¹⁶They shall hunger no more, neither thirst anymore;

the sun shall not strike them,

nor any scorching heat.

¹⁷For the Lamb in the midst of the throne will be their shepherd,

and he will guide them to springs of living water,

and God will wipe away every tear from their eyes."

Go Deeper

If the scroll is filled with such terrible judgments, why does it need to be opened in the first place? Wouldn't it be better to leave it sealed? Consider, however, that if we, who are such poor judges of justice, long to see a day when all is made right, how much more so the Holy and Just God of the universe?

The scroll belongs to God who composed its contents—specifically God the Father. When Jesus was asked about certain details about the end, He said, "But concerning that day and hour no one knows, not even the angels of heaven, nor the Son, but the Father only" (Matt. 24:36). The Lamb can break the seals because of His special role in salvation (Rev. 5:9–14). Apart from the Lamb's sacrifice, the world would be utterly destroyed. The final judgments of God on the world, as terrible as they may be, are still filtered through the grace and mercy He demonstrated at the cross and continues to offer people today.

I n chapter 5, John reported a profound moment of truth. As a new arrival to heaven, he wasn't used to the way things are done there. When the "strong angel" proclaimed the question, "Who is worthy to open the scroll and break its seals?" (Rev. 5:2), John instantly concluded that if there was doubt in this place, then all hope was lost. That thought overwhelmed him, and he began to "weep loudly" (v. 4). But one of the elders told him to stop weeping and "behold, the Lion of the tribe of Judah" (v. 5).

At this point John noticed, not a Lion but "a Lamb standing, as though it had been slain" (v. 6). The Lamb had visible signs of suffering but was very much alive. Before we wonder too much about this we ought to remember that Jesus bore in His resurrected body the marks of His sacrifice on the cross—wounded hands and side. John was looking at the glorified Christ.

Jesus' humble appearance is just one more reminder of the Father's wonderful promise: "Therefore God has highly exalted him and bestowed on him the name that is above every name, so that at the name of Jesus every knee should bow, in heaven and on earth and under the earth, and every tongue confess that Jesus Christ is Lord, to the glory of God the Father" (Phil. 2:9–11).

When the Lamb took the scroll from the One "seated on the throne" (Rev. 5:7), all heaven broke out in an explosion of praise which included "bowls full of incense, which are the prayers of the

" *Understanding the Gospel makes us responsible. We risk eternal separation from God if we delay our response. Christ may come at any time.* **"**

saints" (v. 8). God's throne room reverberated with wave after wave of voices singing "a new song" (v. 9).

John used chapter 6 to describe what happened when the Lamb broke each of the first six seals. With each broken seal the scroll was allowed to unroll further and reveal the contents hidden inside.

The cracking of seals one through four released the four horse-men of the Apocalypse, each representing a form of judgment. The first was a seemingly invincible figure on a white horse who con-quered and crushed. Next rode a figure on a red horse who unleashed war and killing. Then came a black horse whose rider brought famine on the earth. Last rode Death on a pale horse accom-panied by Hades to devastate a quarter of the earth's population.

Seal number five revealed to John "the souls of those who had been slain for the word of God and for the witness they had borne" (6:9). Seal six followed God's promise of judgment delayed "a little longer" (v. 11) and unleashed an indescribable natural disaster on earth (vv. 12–17). Sun, moon and stars changed appearances, mete-ors showered the earth and people in terror of judgment begged for death.

Before the Lamb cracks the seventh seal in chapter 8, chapter 7 provides a "time-out." John watches as two large groups are identi-fied for special treatment.

One group is made up exclusively of Jews—144,000 descendants of the 12 tribes. The process of breaking the seals on the scroll gets interrupted for the "sealing" of these 144,000 "servants of our God" (7:3). The other group is a countless multitude "from every nation, from all tribes and peoples and languages" (v. 9). An elder informed John that these are people who have come to faith during the Tribulation and have suffered death for believing in Christ. They are not people who witnessed the snatching away of the Church (the Rapture) and finally decided they should believe in Christ, for 2 Thessalonians 2:11–12 makes that impossible. Those who have rejected Christ will be completely fooled by the Antichrist and will remain in their unbelief. But many who have not known the Gospel at the time of the Rapture will turn to Christ afterward.

Understanding the Gospel makes us responsible. We risk eternal separation from God if we delay our response. Christ may come at any time. As Paul expressed so urgently, "Be reconciled to God.... For he says, 'In a favorable time I listened to you, and in a day of salvation I have helped you.' Behold, now is the favorable time; behold, now is the day of salvation" (2 Cor. 5:20, 6:2). If you want to see the glorified Christ in the future, you must trust Him as your crucified Savior today.

Express It

Those who are saved out of the tribulation will declare before the throne, "Salvation belongs to our God who sits on the throne, and to the Lamb!" (Rev. 7:10). Meditate on that phrase before the Lord, and express to Him in prayer what those words about Him mean to you.

Consider It

As you read Revelation 6:1–7:17, consider these questions:

1) What does the invitation "Come!" indicate about who is in control of the final events of history?

2) Who does the first rider on a white horse represent?

3) How does the rider of the black horse (6:5–6) demonstrate his power of famine?

4) What are the six catastrophic events that occur with the cracking of the sixth seal?

5) If only the Lamb can open the seals on the scroll of history, what does that tell you about the seal placed on the "servants of God" mentioned in 7:2–14?

6) How would you describe the present condition of your relationship with God? Are you sealed in Christ?

7) When you think about the future, in what ways does the Book of Revelation affect your attitude and outlook?

Judgment and Witness

Possibly one of the most shocking images in Revelation is not the terrible judgments, but the hardened hearts of those who witness them. By seeing a glimpse of these terrible events through this lesson, you have the chance now to examine where your heart is.

Revelation 8:1–11:19

The Seventh Seal and the Golden Censer

8When the Lamb opened the seventh seal, there was silence in heaven for about half an hour. [2]Then I saw the seven angels who stand before God, and seven trumpets were given to them. [3]And another angel came and stood at the altar with a golden censer, and he was given much incense to offer with the prayers of all the saints on the golden altar before the throne, [4]and the smoke of the incense, with the prayers of the saints, rose before God from the hand of the angel. [5]Then the angel took the censer and filled it with fire from the altar and threw it on the earth, and there were peals of thunder, rumblings, flashes of lightning, and an earthquake.

The Seven Trumpets

[6]Now the seven angels who had the seven trumpets prepared to blow them.

[7]The first angel blew his trumpet, and there followed hail and fire, mixed with blood, and these were thrown upon the earth. And a third of the earth was burned up, and a third of the trees were burned up, and all green grass was burned up.

[8]The second angel blew his trumpet, and something like a great mountain, burning with fire, was thrown into the sea, and a third of the sea became blood. [9]A third of the living creatures in the sea died, and a third of the ships were destroyed.

[10]The third angel blew his trumpet, and a great star fell from heaven, blazing like a torch, and it fell on a third of the rivers and on the springs of water. [11]The name of the star is Wormwood. A third of the waters became wormwood, and many people died from the water, because it had been made bitter.

[12]The fourth angel blew his trumpet, and a third of the sun was struck, and a third of the moon, and a third of the stars, so that a third of their light might be darkened, and a third of the day might be kept from shining, and likewise a third of the night.

[13]Then I looked, and I heard an eagle crying with a loud voice as it flew directly overhead, "Woe, woe, woe to those who dwell on the earth, at the blasts of the other trumpets that the three angels are about to blow!"

9And the fifth angel blew his trumpet, and I saw a star fallen from heaven to earth, and he was given the key to the shaft of the bottomless pit. [2]He opened the shaft of the bottomless pit, and from the shaft rose smoke like the smoke of a great furnace, and the sun and the air were darkened with the smoke from the shaft. [3]Then from the smoke came locusts on the earth, and they were given power like the power of scorpions of the earth. [4]They were told not to harm the grass of the earth or any green plant or any tree, but only those people who do not have the seal of God on their foreheads. [5]They were allowed to torment them for five months, but not to kill them, and their torment was like the torment of a scorpion when it stings someone. ⁶And in those days people will seek death and will not find it. They will long to die, but death will flee from them.

⁷In appearance the locusts were like horses prepared for battle: on their heads were what looked like crowns of gold; their faces were like human faces, ⁸their hair like women's hair, and their teeth like lions' teeth; ⁹they had breastplates like breastplates of iron, and the noise of their wings was like the noise of many chariots with horses rushing into battle. ¹⁰They have tails and stings like scorpions, and their power to hurt people for five months is in their tails. ¹¹They have as king over them the angel of the bottomless pit. His name in Hebrew is Abaddon, and in Greek he is called Apollyon.

¹²The first woe has passed; behold, two woes are still to come.

¹³Then the sixth angel blew his trumpet, and I heard a voice from the four horns of the golden altar before God, ¹⁴saying to the sixth angel who had the trumpet, "Release the four angels who are bound at the great river Euphrates." ¹⁵So the four angels, who had been prepared for the hour, the day, the month, and the year, were released to kill a third of mankind. ¹⁶The number of mounted troops was twice ten thousand times ten thousand; I heard their number. ¹⁷And this is how I saw the horses in my vision and those who rode them: they wore breastplates the color of fire and of sapphire and of sulfur, and the heads of the horses were like lions'

heads, and fire and smoke and sulfur came out of their mouths. ¹⁸By these three plagues a third of mankind was killed, by the fire and smoke and sulfur coming out of their mouths. ¹⁹For the power of the horses is in their mouths and in their tails, for their tails are like serpents with heads, and by means of them they wound.

²⁰The rest of mankind, who were not killed by these plagues, did not repent of the works of their hands nor give up worshiping demons and idols of gold and silver and bronze and stone and wood, which cannot see or hear or walk, ²¹nor did they repent of their murders or their sorceries or their sexual immorality or their thefts.

The Angel and the Little Scroll

10Then I saw another mighty angel coming down from heaven, wrapped in a cloud, with a rainbow over his head, and his face was like the sun, and his legs like pillars of fire. ²He had a little scroll open in his hand. And he set his right foot on the sea, and his left foot on the land, ³and called out with a loud voice, like a lion roaring. When he called out, the seven thunders sounded. ⁴And when the seven thunders had sounded, I was about to write, but I heard a voice from heaven saying, "Seal up what the seven thunders have said, and do not write it down." ⁵And the angel whom I saw standing on the sea and on the land raised his right hand to heaven ⁶and swore by him who lives forever and ever, who created heaven and what is in it, the earth and what is in it, and the sea and what is in it, that there would be no more delay, ⁷but that in the days of the trumpet call to be sounded by the seventh angel, the mystery of God would be fulfilled, just as he announced to his servants the prophets.

[8]Then the voice that I had heard from heaven spoke to me again, saying, "Go, take the scroll that is open in the hand of the

> # Key Verse
>
> *"We give thanks to you, Lord God Almighty, who is and who was, for you have taken your great power and begun to reign"* (Rev. 11:17).

angel who is standing on the sea and on the land." [9]So I went to the angel and told him to give me the little scroll. And he said to me, "Take and eat it; it will make your stomach bitter, but in your mouth it will be sweet as honey." [10]And I took the little scroll from the hand of the angel and ate it. It was sweet as honey in my mouth, but when I had eaten it my stomach was made bitter. [11]And I was told, "You must again prophesy about many peoples and nations and languages and kings."

The Two Witnesses

11Then I was given a measuring rod like a staff, and I was told, "Rise and measure the temple of God and the altar and those who worship there, [2]but do not measure the court outside the temple; leave that out, for it is given over to the nations, and they will trample the holy city for forty-two months. [3]And I

will grant authority to my two witnesses, and they will prophesy for 1,260 days, clothed in sackcloth."

[4]These are the two olive trees and the two lampstands that stand before the Lord of the earth. [5]And if anyone would harm them, fire pours from their mouth and consumes their foes. If anyone would harm them, this is how he is doomed to be killed. [6]They have the power to shut the sky, that no rain may fall during the days of their prophesying, and they have power over the waters to turn them into blood and to strike the earth with every kind of plague, as often as they desire. [7]And when they have finished their testimony, the beast that rises from the bottomless pit will make war on them and conquer them and kill them, [8]and their dead bodies will lie in the street of the great city that symbolically is called Sodom and Egypt, where their Lord was crucified. [9]For three and a half days some from the peoples and tribes and languages and nations will gaze at their dead bodies and refuse to let them be placed in a tomb, [10]and those who dwell on the earth will rejoice over them and make merry and exchange presents, because these two prophets had been a torment to those who dwell on the earth. [11]But after the three and a half days a breath of life from God entered them, and they stood up on their feet, and great fear fell on those who saw them. [12]Then they heard a loud voice from heaven saying to them, "Come up here!" And they went up to heaven in a cloud, and their enemies watched them. [13]And at that hour there was a great earthquake, and a tenth of the city fell. Seven thousand people were killed in the

earthquake, and the rest were terrified and gave glory to the God of heaven.

[14]The second woe has passed; behold, the third woe is soon to come.

The Seventh Trumpet

[15]Then the seventh angel blew his trumpet, and there were loud voices in heaven, saying, "The kingdom of the world has become the kingdom of our Lord and of his Christ, and he shall reign forever and ever." [16]And the twenty-four elders who sit on their thrones before God fell on their faces and worshiped God, [17]saying,

"We give thanks to you, Lord God Almighty,

who is and who was,

for you have taken your great power and begun to reign.

[18]The nations raged,

but your wrath came,

and the time for the dead to be judged,

and for rewarding your servants, the prophets and saints,

and those who fear your name,

both small and great,

and for destroying the destroyers of the earth."

[19]Then God's temple in heaven was opened, and the ark of his covenant was seen within his temple. There were flashes of lightning, rumblings, peals of thunder, an earthquake, and heavy hail.

Go Deeper

In chapter 10 John reports a memorable dining experience. An angel appears with a new small scroll. Twice (vv. 2, 8) the scroll is described as "open." But, rather than having a chance to read the scroll, John is told to eat it.

This moment of literary consumption parallels other incidents recorded in God's Word. In the middle of one of his famous complaints, Jeremiah reports, "Your words were found, and I ate them, and your words became to me a joy and the delight of my heart" (Jer. 15:16).

Despite his hardships, Jeremiah couldn't help but appreciate the sweetness of God's Word. Ezekiel described a meal of God's Word (Ezek. 2:8–3:3, 10, 14) that, like John's, was sweet in his mouth.

But God's Word cannot simply be a meal we enjoy. As we consume it, we must apply it to our own lives and share it with others. The bittersweetness comes when we realize at times just how much God's Word may require of us. Note in 2 Timothy 3:16 the four spiritual health benefits of consuming God's Word. Some might give us a slight "upset stomach" in life. How healthy are your eating habits when it comes to God's Word?

Our last lesson ended with one seal still intact on the great scroll the Lamb was holding. The previous six seals led to calamities on earth. Unexpectedly, the breaking of the seventh seal resulted in utter silence in God's throne room (Rev. 8:1). This is the eye of the storm of judgment. For a half hour, heaven held its breath, and seven trumpet-playing angels prepared to announce further consequences on our planet.

In a legal sense, the seals represent the conviction stage of the trial of humanity. Now comes the sentencing stage. The proceedings continued when all were brought to attention by an angel who threw a large censer of holy fire on the earth, causing "thunder, rumblings, flashes of lightning, and an earthquake" (v. 5).

As with the seals, six of the trumpets blew in succession, followed by a pause (8:6—9:21). The first trumpet announced a firestorm that scorched a third of the earth. Trees and plant life were the primary targets. Where grass once grew, only blackened soil remained.

When the second trumpet sounded, a huge burning body fell into the sea, killing a third of the marine life, sinking thousands of ships and turning the sea to blood. The third trumpet sounded, and a third of the planet's drinking water became poisoned. At the sound of trumpet four, the sun (and consequently the moon) lost a third of its light-producing power. A third of the stars disappeared from the night sky. These first four trumpet blasts seem to occur almost simultaneously, as these devastating effects overlap.

At this point an eagle alerted John that the last three trumpets would announce terrible judgment on "those who dwell on the earth" (8:13). Whereas the first four trumpets signaled calamities on the environment (land, sea, fresh water and sky), the last three would announce direct punishment on sinful humanity. Repeating "woe" three times not only indicates the terror about to fall on the earth, but also lets us know that heaven takes no glee in the fate of the world.

When the fifth trumpet blew, a living star, later identified as

> *" Given John's vivid prophecy, who would want to delay trusting Christ? What reason would be good enough to make us say 'No' to the One who has provided us with the gift of forgiveness and eternal life? "*

Satan (9:1,11), unlocked the bottomless pit and released a plague of gruesome, ravaging locusts. Their description (9:7–10) leaves little doubt that they were demons in temporary visible form. They left vegetation unharmed but tormented people with agonizing stings. Their venom caused agony, but not death. They could not attack those who "have the seal of God on their foreheads" (9:4). Their king is Lucifer, the fallen star (compare 9:1 with Isa. 14:12–15), and their reign of terror lasts "five months" (Rev 9:10).

The sixth angel blows his trumpet and unleashes a vast cavalry that marches from east to west, crossing the river Euphrates, in modern-day Iraq. John reports their number at 200 million strong, and they kill a third of the human population. The way he describes their arsenal reads a lot like an ancient attempt to say "chemical and biological weapons." (See vv. 9:17–19.)

Despite the severity of suffering inflicted on the world, those who survived to this point and who had not already surrendered to God displayed a remarkable united response. They refused to repent (9:20–21). They continued to worship spirits and objects they had chosen as gods. They had no hope, but remained stubbornly sinful. Much like the effects of the plagues on Egypt in Exodus, the last plagues on the earth were met with hardened human hearts.

Chapter 10 and most of 11 of Revelation record an interlude between trumpets six and seven. The episode began with a small scroll and seven thunders. When John tried to write what he heard, he was forbidden. Instead, the angel gave him the scroll with instructions to eat it and a warning that it would taste sweet but turn sour in his stomach.

John's commission to prophesy was renewed at this point, and we are introduced to two characters who are active throughout this period—the two witnesses who prophesy on earth for three-and-a-half years. When they "finished their testimony" (11:7), God allowed them to be killed only to raise them again three-and-a-half days later and remove them to heaven. Even during the Great Tribulation, no one can claim God has not offered people abundant opportunities to repent, and yet the death of these faithful servants of God signals a global celebration by the same hardened hearts described at the end of the sixth trumpet's aftershocks.

When the seventh trumpet sounds, the immediate effect occurs in heaven. Not the silence that followed the seventh seal but an outburst of worship (11:15–18). The first half of the Tribulation ends with praise for the glorified Christ who "shall reign forever and ever" (11:15). Given John's vivid prophecy, who would want to delay trusting Christ? What reason would be good enough to make us say "No" to the One who has provided us with the gift of forgiveness and eternal life?

Express It

Turn to Revelation 11:17–18 and read the prayer aloud.
Use one or more of the phrases to expand into an extended
conversation with God about His purpose in your life and
His plans for the world.

Consider It

As you read Revelation 8:1–11:19, consider these questions:

1) How does John describe the incense that fills the angel's golden censer (8:3–4)?

2) Which of the first four trumpets (8:6–12) announces a catastrophe that most directly impacts human life?

3) Why does the eagle cry, "Woe, woe, woe," in 8:13?

4) What makes the "locusts" (9:3–11) particularly loathsome as far as you're concerned? Why?

5) How do you explain the response of the survivors of the calamities to this point in the Tribulation, particularly as John describes them in 9:20–21?

6) Who would you say are some of the most outspoken witnesses for Christ on the world scene today?

7) What conclusions have you reached about the experience and effectiveness of the two witnesses whose ministry is described in 11:3–13?

Enter the Antichrist

As long as Christ has been showing His glory on earth, Satan has been trying to steal it. In this lesson, you'll learn how Satan will one day make the ultimate deception and how you can see through his lies today.

Revelation 12:1–13:10

The Woman and the Dragon

12And a great sign appeared in heaven: a woman clothed with the sun, with the moon under her feet, and on her head a crown of twelve stars. [2]She was pregnant and was crying out in birth pains and the agony of giving birth. [3]And another sign appeared in heaven: behold, a great red dragon, with seven heads and ten horns, and on his heads seven diadems. [4]His tail swept down a third of the stars of heaven and cast them to the earth. And the dragon stood before the woman who was about to give birth, so that when she bore her child he might devour it. [5]She gave birth to a male child, one who is to rule all the nations with a rod of iron, but her child was caught up to God and to his throne, [6]and the woman fled into the wilderness, where she has a place prepared by God, in which she is to be nourished for 1,260 days.

Satan Thrown Down to Earth

[7]Now war arose in heaven, Michael and his angels fighting against the dragon. And the dragon and his angels fought back, [8]but he was defeated and there was no longer any place for them in heaven. [9]And the great dragon was thrown down, that ancient serpent, who is called the devil and Satan, the deceiver of the whole world—he was thrown down to the earth, and his angels were thrown down with him. [10]And I heard a loud voice in heaven, saying, "Now the salvation and the power and the kingdom of our God and the authority of his Christ have come, for the accuser of our brothers has been thrown down, who accuses them day and night before our God. [11]And they have conquered him by the blood of the Lamb and by the word of their testimony, for they loved not their lives even unto death. [12]Therefore, rejoice, O heavens and you who dwell in them! But woe to you, O earth and sea, for the devil has come down to you in great wrath, because he knows that his time is short!"

[13]And when the dragon saw that he had been thrown down to the earth, he pursued the woman who had given birth to the male child. [14]But the woman was given the two wings of the great eagle so that she might fly from the serpent into the wilderness, to the place where she is to be nourished for a time, and times, and half a time. [15]The serpent poured water like a river out of his mouth after the woman, to sweep her away with a flood. [16]But the earth came to the help of the woman, and the earth opened its mouth and swallowed the river that the dragon had poured from his mouth. [17]Then the dragon became furious with the woman and went off to make war on the rest of her offspring, on those who keep the commandments of God and hold to the testimony of Jesus. And he stood on the sand of the sea.

The First Beast

13And I saw a beast rising out of the sea, with ten horns and seven heads, with ten diadems on its horns and blasphemous names on its heads. [2]And the beast that I saw was like a leopard; its feet were like a bear's, and its mouth was like a lion's mouth. And to it the dragon gave his power and his throne and great authority. [3]One of its heads seemed to have a mortal wound, but its mortal wound was healed, and the whole earth marveled as they followed the beast. [4]And they worshiped the dragon, for he had given his authority to the beast, and they worshiped the beast, saying, "Who is like the beast, and who can fight against it?"

[5]And the beast was given a mouth uttering haughty and blasphemous words, and it was allowed to exercise authority for forty-two months. [6]It opened its mouth to utter blasphemies against God, blaspheming his name and his dwelling, that is, those who dwell in heaven. [7]Also it was allowed to make war on the saints and to conquer them. And authority was given it over every tribe and people and language and nation, [8]and all who dwell on earth will worship it, everyone whose name has not been written before the foundation of the world in the book of life of the Lamb that was slain. [9]If anyone has an ear, let him hear:

[10]If anyone is to be taken captive,

to captivity he goes;

if anyone is to be slain with the sword,

with the sword must he be slain.

Here is a call for the endurance and faith of the saints.

> # Key Verse
>
> *And they worshiped the dragon, for he had given his authority to the beast, and they worshiped the beast, saying, "Who is like the beast, and who can fight against it?"* (Rev. 13:4).

Go Deeper

The glorified Christ sneaks up on us. He certainly took the dragon by surprise on that night in Bethlehem. Back then there were lots of people "waiting" for a messiah (savior)—but the wrong kind of messiah. They were looking for a savior from their oppressors, not a Savior from their sins.

The tendency to look for the wrong answer runs deep in us. That's why many people will be fooled by the false "messiah" who comes in the future. Satan will give them the savior they *think* they need instead of the Savior they really need.

In all likelihood, the glorified Christ took you by surprise. He seems to do this even when we're looking for Him. Elsewhere, when John was trying to describe this "surprise effect" Jesus has, he used the term, "glory."

(continue)

"And the Word became flesh and dwelt among us, and we have seen his glory, glory as of the only Son from the Father, full of grace and truth" (John 1:14). If you aren't sure you have seen the glory of Christ, it's probably time to get to know Him better!

The Book of Revelation offers us understanding about the future, but it also helps us grasp the past. Spiritual warfare has been raging since the dawn of time. We chose sides through our ancestors in the garden when they listened to the serpent and disobeyed God. Each of us has since endorsed that decision with our own sins.

But God didn't give up on us. He has taken into account the schemes of Satan even as He has worked out the salvation He offers to mankind. In chapter 12 of Revelation, John reports the panorama of history that he was shown in the aftermath of the seventh trumpet.

In the opening scene, John saw a symbolic pregnant woman who represents Israel and reminds us of God's promise to deliver a Savior to the world through her. That promise was fulfilled when Jesus was born. Satan, the dragon in the scene, was determined to devour the child at birth. The way Jesus arrived caught Satan by surprise, and he was always several steps behind God's moves throughout Jesus' life on earth.

From the killing of the children of Bethlehem to the killing of Jesus on the cross, every time Satan thought he had gained the upper hand, he was defeated again. In John's vision, not only was the "child" removed by God (as Jesus was in His ascension), but the woman (Israel) was sheltered from the dragon in the wilderness for the last three-and-a-half years of the Tribulation.

At verse 12:7, the scene abruptly shifts from earth to heaven, which means "the heavens" or the atmosphere. There a war rages between God's angelic army led by Michael and Satan's army of fallen angels. The defeat of Satan leads to a further fall, and they are "thrown down to the earth" (v. 9). This moment of victory is celebrated with a reminder that any defeat of Satan occurs through the blood of the Lamb. Revelation 12:11 describes the way we ultimately con-

"No matter how hard Satan tries, he cannot dim the glory of Jesus. People may close their eyes or turn their backs, but neither of those actions reduces Jesus' divine stature."

quer Satan's attacks against us: "And they have conquered him by the blood of the Lamb and by the word of their testimony, for they loved not their lives even unto death." Our lives are in His hands.

Action now returns to earth, where Satan reacts to his downfall and coming detainment (Rev. 20) by renewing his efforts to persecute and destroy the woman (Israel) mentioned at the beginning of chapter 12. Her special protection in the wilderness again gets mentioned. Satan turns his full fury on "those who keep the commandments of God and hold to the testimony of Jesus" (12:17). Those who become Christ-followers in the Tribulation will suffer greatly.

At the end of chapter 12 the historic overview concludes with a return to action in the middle of the Tribulation. The stage is set for the rise of the Antichrist. We see that just as Satan is the "father of lies" (John 8:44), he is also the father of deceptions. If he can't be God, he will pretend to be.

Revelation 13 introduces us to the false trinity: Satan, the Antichrist and the false prophet. As the false father, the Devil arranges for the rise of a false son, the Antichrist (13:1). He is introduced as the "first beast" (v. 12), with a description that makes him both a kingdom and a king. The deception is complete down to the details of a "wounded head" (v. 3), possibly explained as a "false resurrection" to mimic Jesus.

By the end of the chapter (13:18), we know the Antichrist is a man—indicated by the famous number 666. The third member of the false trinity is introduced by the rise of a second beast (13:11–18), someone who exercises spiritual powers on behalf of the first beast. (We will look at his role more fully in the next lesson.)

The Antichrist (beast one) rules with power throughout the earth. His appearance serves as the catalyst for Satan's brief moment of glory as the world bows before him: "And the whole earth marveled as they followed the beast. And they worshiped the dragon, for he had given his authority to the beast, and they worshiped the beast, saying, 'Who is like the beast, and who can fight against it?'" (Rev. 13:3–4).

The Devil's obsession has always been to seek worship—to replace God. The objective in each of his attempts to tempt Jesus in the wilderness (see Matt. 4:1–11) was to get Jesus to "worship" him through obedience (turning stones to bread), independence (taking God's protection for granted) and compromise (gaining the world but forfeiting His soul by bowing before Satan).

No matter how hard Satan tries, he cannot dim the glory of Jesus. People may close their eyes or turn their backs, but neither of those actions reduces Jesus' divine stature. A scan of these chapters may cause us to wonder where the glorified Christ is in all this demonic chaos, but a closer look shows us He is active, present and still redeeming, protecting and receiving all those whose names have been "written before the foundation of the world in the book of life of the Lamb that was slain" (Rev. 13:8). Those who bow to anyone else are ultimately bowing to Satan's plan. Our worship always reveals our deepest allegiance.

Express It

What is your attitude as you prepare to pray? Many of us dread prayer as an effort requiring attentiveness, patience, and concentration. But prayer isn't just work. Prayer is war. We might think prayer is a time-out from the battle when, in fact, prayer is the battle. If we think of prayer as work, it becomes an issue of lifestyle and convenience. If we think of prayer as warfare, it takes on life-and-death importance. Ask God to help you examine your attitude and preparation when you spend time in His presence.

Consider It

As you read Revelation 12:1–13:10, consider these questions:

1) In what ways does the vision of the woman (12:1–6) remind you of Joseph's vision in Genesis 37:9–10?

2) What examples of Satan's sworn design to destroy as many humans as possible can you find in these two chapters?

3) As you read about Satan's tactics in these two chapters, how does Ephesians 6:10–20 help you deal with them in your life right now?

4) To what degree would you say you are aware of the reality of spiritual warfare? How seriously do you take your role in the conflict?

5) What significance/meaning do you see in each part of the first beast's appearance (13:1–3)?

6) Why do the people described in this chapter readily bow and worship Satan?

7) What is the extent and limit of Satan's permitted authority during this part of the Tribulation?

Lesson
8

The Mark of the Beast

It is never easy to remain strong in our convictions—even more so when Satan is pressing his attack on all sides. As you go through this lesson, you'll discover that God promises you great blessings when you persevere.

Revelation 13:11–14:20

The Second Beast

¹¹Then I saw another beast rising out of the earth. It had two horns like a lamb and it spoke like a dragon. ¹²It exercises all the authority of the first beast in its presence, and makes the earth and its inhabitants worship the first beast, whose mortal wound was healed. ¹³It performs great signs, even making fire come down from heaven to earth in front of people, ¹⁴and by the signs that it is allowed to work in the presence of the beast it deceives those who dwell on earth, telling them to make an image for the beast that was wounded by the sword and yet lived. ¹⁵And it was allowed to give breath to the image of the beast, so that the image of the beast might even speak and might cause those who would not worship the image of the beast to be slain. ¹⁶Also it causes all, both small and great, both rich and poor, both free and slave, to be marked on the right hand or the forehead, ¹⁷so that no one can buy or sell unless he has the mark, that is, the name of the beast or the number of its name. ¹⁸This calls for wisdom: let the one who has understanding calculate the number of the beast, for it is the number of a man, and his number is 666.

The Lamb and the 144,000

14Then I looked, and behold, on Mount Zion stood the Lamb, and with him 144,000 who had his name and his Father's name written on their foreheads. ²And I heard a voice from heaven like the roar of many waters and like the sound of loud thunder. The voice I heard was like the sound of harpists playing on their harps, ³and they were singing a new song before the throne and before the four living creatures and before the elders. No one could learn that song except the 144,000 who had been redeemed from the earth. ⁴It is these who have not defiled themselves with women, for they are virgins. It is these who follow the Lamb wherever he goes. These have been redeemed from mankind as firstfruits for God and the Lamb, ⁵and in their mouth no lie was found, for they are blameless.

The Messages of the Three Angels

⁶Then I saw another angel flying directly overhead, with an eternal gospel to proclaim to those who dwell on earth, to every nation and tribe and language and people. ⁷And he said with a loud voice, "Fear God and give him glory, because the hour of his judgment has come, and worship him who made heaven and earth, the sea and the springs of water."

⁸Another angel, a second, followed, saying, "Fallen, fallen is Babylon the great, she who made all nations drink the wine of the passion of her sexual immorality."

⁹And another angel, a third, followed

them, saying with a loud voice, "If anyone worships the beast and its image and receives a mark on his forehead or on his hand, [10]he also will drink the wine of God's wrath, poured full strength into the cup of his anger, and he will be tormented with fire and sulfur in the presence of the holy angels and in the presence of the Lamb. [11]And the smoke of their torment goes up forever and ever, and they have no rest, day or night, these worshipers of the beast and its image, and whoever receives the mark of its name."

[12]Here is a call for the endurance of the saints, those who keep the commandments of God and their faith in Jesus.

[13]And I heard a voice from heaven saying, "Write this: Blessed are the dead who die in the Lord from now on." "Blessed indeed," says the Spirit, "that they may rest from their labors, for their deeds follow them!"

The Harvest of the Earth

[14]Then I looked, and behold, a white cloud, and seated on the cloud one like a son of man, with a golden crown on his head, and a sharp sickle in his hand. [15]And another angel came out of the temple, calling with a loud voice to him who sat on the cloud, "Put in your sickle, and reap, for the hour to reap has come, for the harvest of the earth is fully ripe." [16]So he who sat on the cloud swung his sickle across the earth, and the earth was reaped.

[17]Then another angel came out of the temple in heaven, and he too had a sharp sickle. [18]And another angel came out from the altar, the angel who has authority over the fire, and he called with a loud voice to the one who had the sharp sickle, "Put in your sickle and gather the clusters from the vine of the earth, for its grapes are ripe." [19]So the angel swung his sickle across the earth and gathered the grape harvest of the earth and threw it into the great winepress of the wrath of God. [20]And the winepress was trodden outside the city, and blood flowed from the winepress, as high as a horse's bridle, for 1,600 stadia.

> # Key Verse
>
> *Here is a call for the endurance of the saints, those who keep the commandments of God and their faith in Jesus* (Rev. 14:12).

Go Deeper

The great harvest described in Revelation 14:14–20 reminds us of several other instances where the Bible speaks of judgment as harvest. In Joel 3:13, describing a future time of God's outpoured Spirit and judgment, God issues a command to, "Put in the sickle, for the harvest is ripe." The next verse makes it clear He is speaking about

(continue

people and their decisions in the "day of the LORD" (3:14), a phrase often used to refer to God's final account-settling with the world.

Turn to Matthew 13:36–43, and you'll find Jesus explaining a parable that He told in 13:24–30 about the wheat and the weeds. Two kinds of people are growing side by side until they are ripe for harvest. Jesus says, "The harvest is the close of the age, and the reapers are angels. Just as the weeds are gathered and burned with fire, so will it be at the close of the age. The Son of Man will send his angels, and they will gather out of his kingdom all causes of sin and all law-breakers, and throw them into the fiery furnace" (Matt. 13:39–42). Whatever age we live in, we are called by the Lord to be both faithful wheat and faithful workers in the harvest. (See Matt. 9:35–38.)

I n the last lesson, we looked at the first two members of the false trinity created by Satan. John described their "revelation" in Chapter 13. The false father, the Devil, arranges for the rise of his false son, the Antichrist. This is followed by the rise of a second beast, a distorted priestly figure who enforces a religion based on the worship of an idol of the first beast.

This third member of the unholy trinity seems to possess miraculous powers, and he uses them to create the life-and-death confrontation that most people think about when they describe the Tribulation. As John puts it, "Also it causes all, both small and great, both rich and poor, both free and slave, to be marked on the right hand or the forehead, so that no one can buy or sell unless he has the mark, that is, the name of the beast or the number of its name" (Rev. 13:16–17). He is describing what is better known as the "mark of the beast."

The number 666 is widely recognized as representing some kind of evil. As is often the case with symbols, several explanations are possible. In the larger context of a book full of sevens, most having to do with God and His judgments, it makes sense to see the repeated six as a multiple way of describing someone or something that falls short of God's perfection. Traditionally, the number for humans is six. Man was created on the sixth day. But the point to emphasize here is the evil intent of the number—to mark those who belong to Satan.

" *Glimpses of the future judgment of God ought to convict us about faithful living. Because we know how the story ends, we have the best reasons to live hopeful lives.* **"**

Two thousand years before bar codes, retinal scans, implanted digital chips and global satellite tracking, a mark on the forehead or hand may have seemed like a crude symbol of allegiance. But we now have the technology that makes this part of John's prophetic vision a relatively simple task. We live in a world of credit cards and other systems that seem to make life easy. But they could just as easily be used to prevent people from getting food and other necessities. We are numbers. We are subject to identity theft by thieves—but what if a world government decided to "own our identities"? Never before have so many pieces of the prophetic puzzle been in place to create a clear picture of real possibilities.

Before the last round of judgments falls on the earth, God provides John with some encouraging glimpses of the big picture. He records these in Revelation 14. In a vivid contrast to the millions who have become subservient to the unholy trinity by the mark of the beast, John sees the Lamb and the 144,000 sealed Jews standing on Mount Zion.

Just when times seem the worst, John sees the glorified Christ. Not only that, but he gets a fast-forward view of the rest of the Tribulation. Three proclaiming angels fly across the sky, each with a different message. The first offers an invitation to all peoples to "fear God and give him glory" (14:7). The second angel announces the fall of Babylon, the capital of the world government (v. 8). The third angel warns that those who worship the beast and receive his mark are destined for punishment (vv. 9–11). Following these warnings, the key verse uses them as a "call for the endurance of the saints" (v. 12).

Those who resist the mark of the beast will do so at the cost of their lives. But, as verse 13 makes clear, they will also be blessed—blessed indeed. This interlude ends with a preview of Armageddon, the great harvest of the last judgment. The grain and the grapes (the population) of the earth will be gathered under a sharp sickle. God will see justice finally done.

The key verse for this lesson calls us to conviction and offers us comfort. Though it is referring to the endurance of the saints during the Tribulation, it also calls believers in every age to endure. That means us too. Glimpses of the future judgment of God ought to convict us about faithful living. Because we know how the story ends, we have the best reasons to live hopeful lives. (See 1 Pet. 3:15.)

In the face of bad news around us, as well as the unavoidable tragedies of life, believers can choose to live with their eyes fixed on Jesus (Heb. 12:1–2). The writer of Hebrews reminds us that we are "surrounded by so great a cloud of witnesses" (12:1). In a very special way, the people who fill the pages of Revelation can serve that same purpose as witnesses from the future in our time if we heed the example their lives provide for us. They do call us to endure, to keep God's commandments and to hold on to our faith in Jesus.

Express It

Use John's experience to shape your prayer today. Ask God to help you never wander to such a place where you would no longer be able to see His glorified Son. Ask Him to open your eyes because you want to see Jesus—always.

Consider It

As you read Revelation 13:11–14:20, consider these questions:

1) In what ways does the second beast mock and mimic the work of the Holy Spirit?

_____

_____

_____

2) How would you handle it if overnight a notice went out that there could be no buying or selling without a pledge of loyalty to a new, all-encompassing government of the world?

_____

_____

_____

3) Why are people taken in by the deception of Satan and his unholy trinity?

_____

_____

_____

4) What seems to be the purpose behind the three proclaiming angels (14:6–11)?

_____

_____

_____

5) Why does the third angel repeat part of his proclamation?

_____

_____

6) What encouragement do you take from this section of Revelation?

_____

_____

_____

7) How does the double blessing of 14:13 strike your soul? How are those believers double-blessed?

_____

_____

_____

Lesson

9

The Bowls of Judgment

It seems almost excessive the way God pours out His wrath on the earth in the last days. But in this lesson, we'll see how to find God's grace even in the midst of His judgment. More importantly, we'll learn to accept that grace before it's too late.

Revelation 15:1–17:18

The Seven Angels with Seven Plagues

15Then I saw another sign in heaven, great and amazing, seven angels with seven plagues, which are the last, for with them the wrath of God is finished.

²And I saw what appeared to be a sea of glass mingled with fire—and also those who had conquered the beast and its image and the number of its name, standing beside the sea of glass with harps of God in their hands. ³And they sing the song of Moses, the servant of God, and the song of the Lamb, saying,

"Great and amazing are your deeds,

O Lord God the Almighty!

Just and true are your ways,

O King of the nations!

⁴Who will not fear, O Lord,

and glorify your name?

For you alone are holy.

All nations will come

and worship you,

for your righteous acts have been

revealed."

⁵After this I looked, and the sanctuary of the tent of witness in heaven was opened, ⁶and out of the sanctuary came the seven angels with the seven plagues, clothed in pure, bright linen, with golden sashes around their chests. ⁷And one of the four living creatures gave to the seven angels seven golden bowls full of the wrath of God who lives forever and ever, ⁸and the sanctuary was filled with smoke from the glory of God and from his power, and no one could enter the sanctuary until the seven plagues of the seven angels were finished.

The Seven Bowls of God's Wrath

16Then I heard a loud voice from the temple telling the seven angels, "Go and pour out on the earth the seven bowls of the wrath of God."

> # Key Verse
>
> *And one of the four living creatures gave to the seven angels seven golden bowls full of the wrath of God who lives forever and ever (Rev. 15:7).*

²So the first angel went and poured out his bowl on the earth, and harmful and painful sores came upon the people who bore the mark of the beast and worshiped its image.

³The second angel poured out his bowl into the sea, and it became like the blood of a corpse, and every living thing died that was in the sea.

⁴The third angel poured out his bowl into the rivers and the springs of water, and they

became blood. [5]And I heard the angel in charge of the waters say,

"Just are you, O Holy One, who is and who was,

for you brought these judgments.

[6]For they have shed the blood of saints and prophets,

and you have given them blood to drink.

It is what they deserve!"

[7]And I heard the altar saying,

"Yes, Lord God the Almighty,

true and just are your judgments!"

[8]The fourth angel poured out his bowl on the sun, and it was allowed to scorch people with fire. [9]They were scorched by the fierce heat, and they cursed the name of God who had power over these plagues. They did not repent and give him glory.

[10]The fifth angel poured out his bowl on the throne of the beast, and its kingdom was plunged into darkness. People gnawed their tongues in anguish [11]and cursed the God of heaven for their pain and sores. They did not repent of their deeds.

[12]The sixth angel poured out his bowl on the great river Euphrates, and its water was dried up, to prepare the way for the kings from the east. [13]And I saw, coming out of the mouth of the dragon and out of the mouth of the beast and out of the mouth of the false prophet, three unclean spirits like frogs. [14]For they are demonic spirits, performing signs, who go abroad to the kings of the whole world, to assemble them for battle on the great day of God the Almighty. [15]("Behold, I am coming like a thief! Blessed is the one who stays awake, keeping his garments on, that he may not go about naked and be seen exposed!") [16]And they assembled them at the place that in Hebrew is called Armageddon.

The Seventh Bowl

[17]The seventh angel poured out his bowl into the air, and a loud voice came out of the temple, from the throne, saying, "It is done!" [18]And there were flashes of lightning, rumblings, peals of thunder, and a great earthquake such as there had never been since man was on the earth, so great was that earthquake. [19]The great city was split into three parts, and the cities of the nations fell, and God remembered Babylon the great, to make her drain the cup of the wine of the fury of his wrath. [20]And every island fled away, and no mountains were to be found. [21]And great hailstones, about one hundred pounds each, fell from heaven on people; and they cursed God for the plague of the hail, because the plague was so severe.

The Great Prostitute and the Beast

17Then one of the seven angels who had the seven bowls came and said to me, "Come, I will show you the judgment of the great prostitute who is seated on many waters, [2]with whom the kings of the earth have committed sexual immorality, and with the wine of whose sexual immorality the dwellers on earth have become drunk." [3]And he carried me away in the Spirit into a wilderness, and I saw a woman sitting on a scarlet beast that was full of blasphemous names, and it had seven heads and ten horns. [4]The woman was arrayed in purple and scarlet, and adorned with gold and jewels and pearls, holding in her hand a golden cup full of abominations and the impurities of her sexual immorality. [5]And on her forehead was written a name of mystery: "Babylon the great, mother of prostitutes and of earth's abominations." [6]And I saw the woman, drunk with the blood of the saints, the blood of the martyrs of Jesus.

When I saw her, I marveled greatly. [7]But the angel said to me, "Why do you marvel? I will tell you the mystery of the woman, and of the beast with seven heads and ten horns that carries her. [8]The beast that you saw was, and is not, and is about to rise from the bottomless pit and go to destruction. And the dwellers on earth whose names have not been written in the book of life from the foundation of the world will marvel to see the beast, because it was and is not and is to come. [9]This calls for a mind with wisdom: the seven heads are seven mountains on which the woman is seated; [10]they are also seven kings, five of whom have fallen, one is, the other has not yet come, and when he does come he must remain only a little while. [11]As for the beast that was and is not, it is an eighth but it belongs to the seven, and it goes to destruction. [12]And the ten horns that you saw are ten kings who have not yet received royal power, but they are to receive authority as kings for one hour, together with the beast. [13]These are of one mind and hand over their power and authority to the beast. [14]They will make war on the Lamb, and the Lamb will conquer them, for he is Lord of lords and King of kings, and those with him are called and chosen and faithful."

[15]And the angel said to me, "The waters that you saw, where the prostitute is seated, are peoples and multitudes and nations and languages. [16]And the ten horns that you saw, they and the beast will hate the prostitute. They will make her desolate and naked, and devour her flesh and burn her up with fire, [17]for God has put it into their hearts to carry out his purpose by being of one mind and handing over their royal power to the beast, until the words of God are fulfilled. [18]And the woman that you saw is the great city that has dominion over the kings of the earth."

Go Deeper

Where do we find the glorified Christ in these three chapters of Revelation? This study has hopefully kept us alert to His presence throughout the book. If what John received was a revelation of Jesus Christ, then we should expect to find Christ revealed on every page. We should be watchful.

In chapter 15, John saw some amazing angels, but he heard the "song of the Lamb" (15:3). The saints who had already

(continued)

given their lives and therefore had "conquered the beast" were gathered for a grand worship service. In chapter 16, John quotes the words of Jesus: "Behold, I am coming like a thief! Blessed is the one who stays awake, keeping his garments on, that he may not go about naked and be seen exposed!" (16:15).

When the Lord appeared to John earlier in the book (3:2–3), He used this same language. But this also refers to an earlier statement Jesus made to his disciples in

---

I n an earlier lesson we drew a comparison between the seals as the conviction part of the trial of humanity (Rev. 6, 8:1). The trumpets then became the sentencing phase of the trial (8:6–9:21, 11:15). In the 15th chapter of Revelation we arrive at the execution segment of the trial. The judgment is finally carried out. Here "the wrath of God is finished" (15:1).

People reading Revelation for the first time often ask at this point, if they haven't already, "Enough! Where's the God of grace, mercy and love that we're used to? Why does God seem so relentless in exercising judgment on the earth?"

Now these are reasonable questions as long as we keep them in context and ask them in humility. We're not in a position to pass judgment on God. In fact, we ought to be asking, "If humanity deserves such wrath, why has God waited so long?"

The answer to all these questions is that God has been relating to His creation under a season or a "dispensation" of grace. That season is coming to an end. God's timing, like everything else about Him, is perfect. There's little point in asking God for an extension of something we didn't deserve in the first place. Salvation arrived at the right time (see Gal. 4:4); so will judgment.

John saw seven angels carrying plagues. Fitting that in the context of plagues, the song sung by those who have conquered the beast through death is the song of Moses. He, too, was a dispenser of plagues when God judged Egypt. Note that each of the plague-carrying angels was also given a bowl of God's wrath. In this way, the plagues become an expression (the final expression) of God's wrath. Sometimes plagues are simply natural consequences for disrespecting the natural systems. If we allow unsanitary conditions to exist in a large city, plagues like typhoid are likely to break out. The plagues

73

Matthew 24:36–44. In Revelation 17, the woman who is Babylon, the worship of Antichrist, was described as drunk with the blood of those faithful to Jesus.

But the tables were turned in 17:14, because Jesus was glorified in this: "They will make war on the Lamb, and the Lamb will conquer them, for he is Lord of lords and King of kings, and those with him are called and chosen and faithful." When all is said and done, Jesus will remain glorified!

John witnessed are direct expressions of God's judgment.

Chapter 16 of Revelation records the pouring out of the bowls of God's wrath upon unrepentant humanity. This apparently occurred in rapid succession, since the effects were cumulative. With each bowl, conditions got worse. First came a bowl that created "harmful and painful sores" (16:2) on those who worshiped the beast. The second bowl transformed the sea into coagulated blood ("of a corpse"), killing what remained of marine life (v. 3).

When the third angel poured out his bowl, the fresh water sources of the world became blood (v. 4). This angel couldn't resist pointing out this was a fitting judgment on those who were so blood-thirsty in their treatment of the "saints and prophets" (v. 6).

The fourth angel poured out his bowl on the sun, but the effects devastated the earth with heat. It was as if God suddenly removed the ozone layer from the planet and people were struck with instant, blistering sunburns. When the fifth angel's bowl plunged the world into darkness, there was no relief in a cool evening. The sores and blisters filled the night with agony. Yet those who were suffering continued to display their hardened hearts. "People gnawed their tongues in anguish and cursed the God of heaven for their pain and sores. They did not repent of their deeds" (vv. 10–11).

Then the sixth angel poured out his bowl, causing the Euphrates River to dry up and a plague of frogs to infest the world. The startling difference between this plague of frogs and the original one of Moses' day in Egypt is the fact that this last-days plague involved only three frogs—three demonic spirits who recruited the vast army gathered at Armageddon for the last stand (vv. 12–16).

The seventh bowl unleashed a storm like no other on the earth. Not only did the sky rain huge hail-boulders, but also a global earth-

> " *God's timing, like everything else about Him, is perfect.... Salvation arrived at the right time; so will judgment.* "

quake erased islands, sank mountains, destroyed cities and split Jerusalem in three. Yet in the darkness John hears the curses of unrepentant people (vv. 17–21). Isn't it amazing that people find it easier to curse God than to believe He exists and loves them?

In the aftermath of the great disaster of the bowl judgments, God provides John with a vision-within-a-vision involving Babylon, the great city that represents the worship of Satan and his representatives on earth. In the chronology of Revelation, what John sees in chapter 17 actually occurs during the first three and a half years of the Tribulation. John's angel-guide explains the figures he sees in his vision. He describes a worldwide religion that rises after the removal of the true church in the Rapture.

This religion is unified by a common hatred for anything or anyone faithful to Jesus Christ. Efforts around the world today to "clarify" Christianity and meld it with other religious systems, which are called "equally sincere and valid," seem to be preparing the way for Revelation 17. Ironically (see 17:15–17) Satan eventually betrays and destroys this religious organization because he is entirely bent on ruling the world.

Express It

As you pray today, mentally list some of the people closest to you who have not yet come to faith in Jesus Christ. Pray for them by name. Ask God if there is anything you can do or say that He might use to draw them to Himself. Then sit quietly for a while and let God tell you what He wants you to do.

Consider It

As you read Revelation 15:1–17:18, consider these questions:

1) What do you learn about God's holiness and wrath in chapter 15?

_____

_____

_____

2) If you had to use only Revelation 15 to explain worship to someone, what would you say?

_____

_____

_____

3) How do the judgments poured out in chapter 16 compare to the previous judgments of the seals and the trumpets?

_____

_____

_____

4) What clues do you find in chapter 17 that tell you the vision is about an anti-God religious system?

_____

_____

5) Looking at the reaction of humankind to the disasters in chapter 16, what does this tell you about responding to God when bad things happen?

_____

_____

6) Why do you think people today (like the people described in Revelation) tend to gravitate to any religious view that avoids wholehearted commitment to Jesus Christ?

_____

_____

_____

7) What are the two or three most compelling reasons why you should remain faithful to Christ?

_____

_____

_____

The Final Battle— Armageddon

In this lesson, we see the final moments on earth; at one time beautiful in the coming of Jesus, yet tragic in that so many refuse to believe in Him. But realize that that day is not here yet—God is still extending His hand of mercy.

Revelation 18:1–19:21

The Fall of Babylon

18After this I saw another angel coming down from heaven, having great authority, and the earth was made bright with his glory. ²And he called out with a mighty voice,

"Fallen, fallen is Babylon the great!

She has become a dwelling place for demons,

a haunt for every unclean spirit,

a haunt for every unclean bird,

a haunt for every unclean and detestable beast.

³For all nations have drunk

the wine of the passion of her sexual immorality,

and the kings of the earth have committed immorality with her,

and the merchants of the earth have grown rich from the power of her luxurious living."

⁴Then I heard another voice from heaven saying,

"Come out of her, my people,

lest you take part in her sins,

lest you share in her plagues;

⁵for her sins are heaped high as heaven,

and God has remembered her iniquities.

⁶Pay her back as she herself has paid back others,

and repay her double for her deeds;

mix a double portion for her in the cup she mixed.

⁷As she glorified herself and lived in luxury,

so give her a like measure of torment and mourning,

since in her heart she says,

'I sit as a queen,

I am no widow,

and mourning I shall never see.'

⁸For this reason her plagues will come in a single day,

death and mourning and famine,

and she will be burned up with fire;

for mighty is the Lord God who has judged her."

⁹And the kings of the earth, who committed sexual immorality and lived in luxury with her, will weep and wail over her when they see the smoke of her burning. ¹⁰They will stand far off, in fear of her torment, and say,

"Alas! Alas! You great city,

you mighty city, Babylon!

For in a single hour your judgment has come."

¹¹And the merchants of the earth weep and mourn for her, since no one buys their cargo anymore, ¹²cargo of gold, silver, jewels, pearls, fine linen, purple cloth, silk, scarlet

cloth, all kinds of scented wood, all kinds of articles of ivory, all kinds of articles of costly wood, bronze, iron and marble, [13]cinnamon, spice, incense, myrrh, frankincense, wine, oil, fine flour, wheat, cattle and sheep, horses and chariots, and slaves, that is, human souls.

[14]"The fruit for which your soul longed
has gone from you,
and all your delicacies and your splendors
are lost to you,
never to be found again!"

[15]The merchants of these wares, who gained wealth from her, will stand far off, in fear of her torment, weeping and mourning aloud,

[16]"Alas, alas, for the great city
that was clothed in fine linen,
in purple and scarlet,
adorned with gold,
with jewels, and with pearls!

[17]For in a single hour all this wealth has
been laid waste."

And all shipmasters and seafaring men, sailors and all whose trade is on the sea, stood far off [18]and cried out as they saw the smoke of her burning,

"What city was like the great city?"

[19]And they threw dust on their heads as they wept and mourned, crying out,

"Alas, alas, for the great city
where all who had ships at sea
grew rich by her wealth!

For in a single hour she has been laid
waste.

[20]Rejoice over her, O heaven,
and you saints and apostles and
prophets,
for God has given judgment for you against
her!"

[21]Then a mighty angel took up a stone like a great millstone and threw it into the sea, saying,

"So will Babylon the great city be thrown
down with violence,
and will be found no more;
[22]and the sound of harpists and musicians, of flute players and trumpeters,
will be heard in you no more,
and a craftsman of any craft
will be found in you no more,
and the sound of the mill
will be heard in you no more,
[23]and the light of a lamp
will shine in you no more,
and the voice of bridegroom and bride
will be heard in you no more,

Key Verse

Then I saw heaven opened, and behold, a white horse! The one sitting on it is called Faithful and True, and in righteousness he judges and makes war (Rev. 19:11).

for your merchants were the great ones of
the earth,

and all nations were deceived by your
sorcery.

24And in her was found the blood of
prophets and of saints,

and of all who have been slain on
earth."

Rejoicing in Heaven

19After this I heard what seemed to be
the loud voice of a great multitude in heaven,
crying out,

"Hallelujah!

Salvation and glory and power belong to
our God,

2for his judgments are true and just;

for he has judged the great prostitute

who corrupted the earth with her
immorality,

and has avenged on her the blood of his
servants."

3Once more they cried out,

"Hallelujah!

The smoke from her goes up forever and
ever."

4And the twenty-four elders and the four
living creatures fell down and worshiped God
who was seated on the throne, saying,
"Amen. Hallelujah!" 5And from the throne
came a voice saying,

"Praise our God,

all you his servants,

you who fear him,

small and great."

The Marriage Supper of the Lamb

6Then I heard what seemed to be the voice
of a great multitude, like the roar of many
waters and like the sound of mighty peals of
thunder, crying out,

"Hallelujah!

For the Lord our God

the Almighty reigns.

7Let us rejoice and exult

and give him the glory,

for the marriage of the Lamb has come,

and his Bride has made herself ready;

8it was granted her to clothe herself

with fine linen, bright and pure"—

for the fine linen is the righteous deeds of
the saints.

9And the angel said to me, "Write this:
Blessed are those who are invited to the marriage supper of the Lamb." And he said to
me, "These are the true words of God."
10Then I fell down at his feet to worship him,
but he said to me, "You must not do that! I
am a fellow servant with you and your brothers who hold to the testimony of Jesus.
Worship God." For the testimony of Jesus is
the spirit of prophecy.

The Rider on a White Horse

11Then I saw heaven opened, and behold,
a white horse! The one sitting on it is called
Faithful and True, and in righteousness he
judges and makes war. 12His eyes are like a
flame of fire, and on his head are many
diadems, and he has a name written that no
one knows but himself. 13He is clothed in a

robe dipped in blood, and the name by which he is called is The Word of God. [14]And the armies of heaven, arrayed in fine linen, white and pure, were following him on white horses. [15]From his mouth comes a sharp sword with which to strike down the nations, and he will rule them with a rod of iron. He will tread the winepress of the fury of the wrath of God the Almighty. [16]On his robe and on his thigh he has a name written, King of kings and Lord of lords.

[17]Then I saw an angel standing in the sun, and with a loud voice he called to all the birds that fly directly overhead, "Come, gather for the great supper of God, [18]to eat the flesh of kings, the flesh of captains, the flesh of mighty men, the flesh of horses and their riders, and the flesh of all men, both free and slave, both small and great." [19]And I saw the beast and the kings of the earth with their armies gathered to make war against him who was sitting on the horse and against his army. [20]And the beast was captured, and with it the false prophet who in its presence had done the signs by which he deceived those who had received the mark of the beast and those who worshiped its image. These two were thrown alive into the lake of fire that burns with sulfur. [21]And the rest were slain by the sword that came from the mouth of him who was sitting on the horse, and all the birds were gorged with their flesh.

Go Deeper

The word "hallelujah" is a borrowed Hebrew term. Perhaps it was considered too hard to effectively translate or simply sounded too wonderful to change, so it was lifted (transliterated) into Greek for the New Testament, and then hundreds of languages that have received God's Word around the world. Since most of the New Testament writers were Jews, they were use to worshiping God with that expression.

Hallelujah actually represents two ideas—"Praise (Hallel) and God (Jah)." It's a command or invitation often used in the Old Testament at the beginning and end of Psalms. For example, it opens Psalm 111 and 112 and ends Psalm 104 and 105. The term also begins and ends Psalm 106, 113 and 135. Hallelujah expresses a short doxology—a burst of praise to God!

When John, in the Spirit, witnessed "a great multitude in heaven, crying out" (Rev. 19:1) he understood what they were saying. Whatever language they were using, he was able to reproduce it in Greek. But there was at least one word that came from his mother-tongue, Hebrew—Hallelujah! If you know Jesus today, you will be part of that great worship chorus. Won't that be a great moment! And think of this—in heaven's special language you already know at least one word: Hallelujah! Get used to using it now!

While Revelation 17 described the rise and fall of the religious aspects of Babylon, chapter 18 deals with the political and economic shell left over when the worldwide religious structure she represents is defeated and destroyed by the Antichrist who no longer needs her.

Without the religious organization and buying power of the global church, compounded by the disastrous worldwide ecological problems, the merchants of the world have a rapidly shrinking market. The one-leader control offered by the Antichrist is quickly collapsing into one big mess. And this chapter catalogs the breakdown. Babylon, the beacon of a golden, godless future, has suddenly become a wasteland. Those who profited by cornering the markets after the removal of the true church express their grief, not over sin, but over their impending bankruptcy.

The last four verses of chapter 18 signal a dramatic shift in the tone of Revelation. The curtain is falling on the old world and this age. It's time for heaven to rejoice. Like a public declaration of condemnation before a huge building is demolished, an angel lifts a massive rock and drops it in the sea. He declares Babylon uninhabitable. In her there will be no longer any signs of life. She is stained by the "blood of prophets and of saints, and of all who have been slain on earth" (v. 24), and that offense has sealed her fate.

Revelation 19 is the Hallelujah Chorus of the New Testament. This chapter includes the only four uses of this great praise word in the New Testament. There's a longstanding tradition that when the audience hears the first strains of the Hallelujah Chorus in Handel's *Messiah*, they rise to their feet in solemn agreement with the message of the song. So, too, when we read this chapter, we ought to feel our hearts and souls leap in anticipation. God is worthy of our highest praise. (See this lesson's **Going Deeper** section.)

The hallelujahs John heard created an opening fanfare for the wedding supper of the Lamb (19:6–10) and the grand entrance of the glorified Christ, the rider on a white horse (19:11–21). John was witnessing a preview of the Second Coming of Jesus Christ. He "saw heaven opened" (19:11) in such a way that "every eye will see him" (1:7). His appearance was as stunning as when John saw Him in the first chapter of this book.

" There's a longstanding tradition that when the audience hears the first strains of the Hallelujah Chorus in Handel's Messiah, *they rise to their feet in solemn agreement with the message of the song. So, too, when we read this chapter, we ought to feel our hearts and souls leap in anticipation. God is worthy of our highest praise. "*

Every title and every aspect of Jesus' arrival for the final battle highlighted some aspect of His glory as King of kings and Lord of lords: Faithful, True, Word of God and even a name only He knows (19:12). Every action taken by Jesus highlighted His unique role: Righteous Judge, Warrior, Wearer of the robe dipped in blood (His sacrifice), Victor and Ruler of nations, and One who treads the furious winepress of God's wrath.

Jesus came as Savior His first time; He arrives as absolute Ruler the second time. Even as His first visit to earth was coming to a close, Jesus announced to Caiaphas the high priest that His role was about to change: "I tell you, from now on you will see the Son of Man seated at the right hand of Power and coming on the clouds of heaven" (Matt. 26:64).

Revelation 19:17–21 describes a battle that turns out to be no fight. The great armies of the earth and the beast gather and are utterly defeated. The two human instruments of Satan in the Tribulation (the beast and the false prophet) who seemed so impressive in power on earth are immediately dispatched "alive into the lake of fire that burns with sulfur" (v. 20).

The sword that comes from Jesus' mouth (vv. 15,21), representing the Word of God, executes God's judgment and kills the army. The final battle will be settled by Jesus' words. "For the word of God is living and active, sharper than any two-edged sword, piercing to the division of soul and of spirit, of joints and of marrow, and discerning the thoughts and intentions of the heart" (Heb. 4:12). At Armageddon, this description of God's Word will be literally demonstrated. And the flesh-eating birds of the world will feast on the remains of the greatest army ever assembled.

Those who are alive in this "in-between" time must take heed to Jesus' words. They decide life or death; eternal life or eternal death. And yet His words for now are filled with hope and invitation: "For God so loved the world, that he gave his only Son, that whoever believes in him should not perish but have eternal life. For God did not send his Son into the world to condemn the world, but in order that the world might be saved through him" (John 3:16–17). When Jesus comes again, this invitation will be rescinded. Then it will be too late.

As you read these words today, if you have never trusted in Jesus as your Savior and Lord, this may be your final opportunity. For, "how shall we escape if we neglect such a great salvation?" (Heb. 2:3).

Express It

After reading chapter 19, the devotion and the **Go Deeper** *section, you should be ready and able to spend some time in prayer and praise. Among other expressions that may come to mind, do your best to finish the following sentence for your Heavenly Father: "Lord, this is what hallelujah means to me today."*

Consider It

As you read Revelation 18:1–19:21, consider these questions:

1) What are the charges that God levels against Babylon in judgment?

_____

_____

2) How did the fall of Babylon affect the political and economic systems of the world? Why?

_____

_____

_____

3) In what ways do the desires for power or wealth influence the way you make decisions?

_____

_____

_____

4) How are the Bride of Christ's preparations described in chapter 19?

_____

_____

_____

5) What should be the results in our lives of the fact that the relationship between Jesus and the Church is called a marriage?

_____

_____

_____

6) What stands out for you the most about Jesus' description as the Rider on the white horse?

_____

_____

_____

7) In what ways does Jesus' role as conquering King and Lord affect your life on a daily basis?

_____

_____

_____

Lesson 11

The Millennial Kingdom

In this amazing picture of the 1,000-year reign of Christ, you will learn that perfect environments don't lead to perfect men and women. Only Christ can make a person perfect and complete, and whether today, or in the Millennium—the choice is still yours.

Revelation 20:1–15

The Thousand Years

20Then I saw an angel coming down from heaven, holding in his hand the key to the bottomless pit and a great chain. 2And he seized the dragon, that ancient serpent, who is the devil and Satan, and bound him for a thousand years, 3and threw him into the pit, and shut it and sealed it over him, so that he might not deceive the nations any longer, until the thousand years were ended. After that he must be released for a little while.

4Then I saw thrones, and seated on them were those to whom the authority to judge was committed. Also I saw the souls of those who had been beheaded for the testimony of Jesus and for the word of God, and who had not worshiped the beast or its image and had not received its mark on their foreheads or their hands. They came to life and reigned with Christ for a thousand years. 5The rest of the dead did not come to life until the thousand years were ended. This is the first resurrection. 6Blessed and holy is the one who shares in the first resurrection! Over such the second death has no power, but they will be priests of God and of Christ, and they will reign with him for a thousand years.

The Defeat of Satan

7And when the thousand years are ended, Satan will be released from his prison 8and will come out to deceive the nations that are at the four corners of the earth, Gog and Magog, to gather them for battle; their number is like the sand of the sea. 9And they marched up over the broad plain of the earth and surrounded the camp of the saints and the beloved city, but fire came down from heaven and consumed them, 10and the devil who had deceived them was thrown into the lake of fire and sulfur where the beast and the false prophet were, and they will be tormented day and night forever and ever.

> # Key Verse
>
> *Blessed and holy is the one who shares in the first resurrection! Over such the second death has no power, but they will be priests of God and of Christ, and they will reign with him for a thousand years* (Rev. 20:6).

The Great White Throne Judgment

11Then I saw a great white throne and him who was seated on it. From his presence earth and sky fled away, and no place was found for them. 12And I saw the dead, great and small, standing before the throne, and books were opened. Then another book was opened, which is the book of life. And the dead were judged by what was written in the books, according to what they had done. [13]And the sea gave up the dead who were in it, Death and Hades gave up the dead who were in them, and they were judged, each one of them, according to what they had done. [14]Then Death and Hades were thrown into the lake of fire. This is the second death, the lake of fire. [15]And if anyone's name was not found written in the book of life, he was thrown into the lake of fire.

Go Deeper

If we are "in Christ," neither the Millennium nor the Last Judgment are particular items of concern for us. After all, we have our hands full with the challenges of our time. We have a King to follow. One of the interesting episodes in the lives of Jesus' first disciples can help us keep the proper perspective.

In Luke 10:1–12 and 17–20, there is a brief account of Jesus commissioning His disciples for ministry. After a short time they return joyfully, amazed that "even the demons are subject to us in your name" (Luke 10:17). Jesus acknowledged the truth of the authority (as Lord of lords) that He had given them. But His concluding statement ought to echo in our hearts and minds every day: "Nevertheless, do not rejoice in this, that the spirits are subject to you, but rejoice that your names are written in heaven" (Luke 10:20).

God has given us powerful glimpses of the future in order for us to live very clearly in the present. Once we have settled the issue of our names written in the Book of Life, we are to keep busy obeying the King who is Life!

The first six verses of Revelation 20 describe the period following the Tribulation and Christ's return, traditionally called the Millennium (a term we've borrowed from Latin that literally means 1,000 years). For many people, this short section is a puzzling parenthesis in the end times.

This is the only passage in the Bible that speaks directly about a literal, 1,000-year reign on earth by Jesus Christ. And although a single mention in Scripture may make something unusual, it doesn't mean we can dismiss it. Six times in six verses the exact time measurement is given. The glorified Lord will bring His kingdom to earth for 1,000 years. While this may present an interpretive challenge for some, let's remember that even the Millennium is a part of God's plan. We can certainly leave the "figuring out how it all works" in His wise hands.

This period begins with the binding and banishment of the dragon (Satan) to the "bottomless pit" (20:1–3). Even here we are warned that he will have one more brief time on the loose to create havoc before he is forever removed (v. 3). With the Devil's departure, the earth returns to an Eden-like state, occupied by those who have remained faithful to Christ and survived the Tribulation. Those martyred during the Tribulation are also raised and reign with Christ (v. 4).

At the beginning of the Millennium, the entire population of the world will be believers in Christ. According to Matthew 13:41–43, 49–50 and 25:41, 46, no unsaved person will enter the reign of Christ. This will be a time of peace that has eluded man since the dawn of time, ruled with "a rod of iron" by the Prince of Peace. This will be a time for fulfillment of such prophecies as Isaiah 2:4: "He shall judge between the nations, and shall decide disputes for many peoples; and they shall beat their swords into plowshares, and their spears into pruning hooks; nation shall not lift up sword against nation, neither shall they learn war anymore."

The peace Jesus establishes will touch the entire created order: "The wolf shall dwell with the lamb, and the leopard shall lie down with the young goat, and the calf and the lion and the fattened calf together; and a little child shall lead them.... The nursing child shall play over the hole of the cobra, and the weaned child shall put his hand on the adder's den" (Isa. 11:6, 8).

" *Yet in that day, as it is in ours, there will be no spiritual grandchildren. The members of each generation must make their own decision about trusting in Jesus as Savior and Lord.* "

But this isn't heaven, and those who are born throughout the next 1,000 years will have the same choice we have had—to surrender to Christ or hold out for our own way. Generations of unbelievers will rise, so that by the time Satan is briefly released at the end of the Millennium, there will be millions eager to side with him. This last rebellion is swiftly terminated by fire and the Devil "who had deceived them was thrown into the lake of fire and sulfur where the beast and the false prophet were, and they will be tormented day and night forever and ever" (Rev. 20:10).

There are at least two huge lessons demonstrated for us by the Millennium events. How can people who are thoroughly committed to Jesus Christ, many of whom have previously given their lives for Him and living under the perfect rule of Christ, raise ungodly children? How can the human race, given a second chance, fail again?

The Millennium shows us that a perfect environment doesn't transform a sinner into a saint. Despite being born into conditions unequaled in peace and opportunity since the Garden of Eden, humans still will choose to rebel. The Millennium also reminds us that faithfulness is not a product of perfect heredity. Babies born during this time period will have believing parents. They will grow up in homes faithful to the King. Yet in that day, as it is in ours, there will be no spiritual grandchildren. The members of each generation must make their own decision about trusting in Jesus as Savior and Lord.

After the Millennium and the cleansing of the universe, John sees the Great White Throne Judgment (20:11–15). This is the final settlement of the matters between God and His creation. Every man, woman and child who has lived will stand before God's throne. The records will be read. The Book of Life will declare the names of those who will spend eternity with Him who is Life. Anyone whose "name was not found written in the book of life, he was thrown into the lake of fire" (v. 15).

Among those things that will be blotted out forever are death and Hades (v. 14). This will be the ultimate fulfillment of the apostle Paul's resurrection prophecy: "Then shall come to pass the saying that is written: 'Death is swallowed up in victory.' 'O death, where is your victory? O death, where is your sting?'" (1 Cor. 15:54–55). If you are trusting in Christ today, you have no reason to fear the great final Judgment.

Express It

We can all think of countless reasons for gratitude to God. When you pray today, practice the discipline that most clearly shows our confidence in the salvation we have in Christ—thanksgiving. When we forget how to be thankful, we begin to lose a sense of security in Christ. We are then likely to start worrying about our "status" with Christ. But regularly thanking God for His gift of salvation helps affirm that we have received it!

Consider It

As you read Revelation 20:1–15, consider these questions:

1) How did John describe the sacrifice made by saints in the tribulation?

_____

_____

_____

2) If Jesus is your King now, how does your life reflect His rule?

_____

_____

_____

3) In contrast with Armageddon, how did God defeat this second great army raised by Satan?

_____

_____

_____

4) Who will be involved in the Great White Throne Judgment?

_____

_____

_____

5) In the final Judgment, what standard will be used? Why?

_____

_____

_____

6) What is the importance of knowing we will be judged for the way we live?

_____

_____

_____

7) When and how was your name written in the Book of Life?

_____

_____

_____

A Tour of the New Jerusalem

In this lesson, you'll get your first glimpse of heaven, and what a wonderful sight it is! Here the old battered earth is remade and the city of God descends to the earth. The sight is one of encouragement for you the believer—the room Jesus promised you is there and cannot be taken away.

Revelation 21:1–27

The New Heaven and the New Earth

21 Then I saw a new heaven and a new earth, for the first heaven and the first earth had passed away, and the sea was no more. ²And I saw the holy city, new Jerusalem, coming down out of heaven from God, prepared as a bride adorned for her husband. ³And I heard a loud voice from the throne saying, "Behold, the dwelling place of God is with man. He will dwell with them, and they will be his people, and God himself will be with them as their God. ⁴He will wipe away every tear from their eyes, and death shall be no more, neither shall there be mourning nor crying nor pain anymore, for the former things have passed away."

⁵And he who was seated on the throne said, "Behold, I am making all things new." Also he said, "Write this down, for these words are trustworthy and true." ⁶And he said to me, "It is done! I am the Alpha and the Omega, the beginning and the end. To the thirsty I will give from the spring of the water of life without payment. ⁷The one who conquers will have this heritage, and I will be his God and he will be my son. ⁸But as for the cowardly, the faithless, the detestable, as for murderers, the sexually immoral, sorcerers, idolaters, and all liars, their portion will be in the lake that burns with fire and sulfur, which is the second death."

The New Jerusalem

⁹Then came one of the seven angels who had the seven bowls full of the seven last plagues and spoke to me, saying, "Come, I will show you the Bride, the wife of the Lamb." ¹⁰And he carried me away in the Spirit to a great, high mountain, and showed me the holy city Jerusalem coming down out of heaven from God, ¹¹having the glory of God, its radiance like a most rare jewel, like a jasper, clear as crystal. ¹²It had a great, high wall, with twelve gates, and at the gates

Key Verse

And he carried me away in the Spirit to a great, high mountain, and showed me the holy city Jerusalem coming down out of heaven from God (Rev. 21:10).

twelve angels, and on the gates the names of the twelve tribes of the sons of Israel were inscribed— ¹³on the east three gates, on the north three gates, on the south three gates, and on the west three gates. ¹⁴And the wall of the city had twelve foundations, and on them were the twelve names of the twelve apostles of the Lamb.

¹⁵And the one who spoke with me had a measuring rod of gold to measure the city and its gates and walls. ¹⁶The city lies foursquare; its length the same as its width. And he measured the city with his rod, 12,000 stadia. Its length and width and height are equal. ¹⁷He also measured its wall, 144 cubits by human measurement, which is also an angel's measurement. ¹⁸The wall was built of jasper, while the city was pure gold, clear as glass. ¹⁹The foundations of the wall of the city were adorned with every kind of jewel. The first was jasper, the second sapphire, the third agate, the fourth emerald, ²⁰the fifth onyx, the sixth carnelian, the seventh chrysolite, the eighth beryl, the ninth topaz, the tenth chrysoprase, the eleventh jacinth, the twelfth amethyst. ²¹And the twelve gates were twelve pearls, each of the gates made of a single pearl, and the street of the city was pure gold, transparent as glass.

²²And I saw no temple in the city, for its temple is the Lord God the Almighty and the Lamb. ²³And the city has no need of sun or moon to shine on it, for the glory of God gives it light, and its lamp is the Lamb. ²⁴By its light will the nations walk, and the kings of the earth will bring their glory into it, ²⁵and its gates will never be shut by day—and there will be no night there. ²⁶They will bring into it the glory and the honor of the nations. ²⁷But nothing unclean will ever enter it, nor anyone who does what is detestable or false, but only those who are written in the Lamb's book of life.

Go Deeper

The glorified Christ will light up New Jerusalem. This fact is so obvious that John mentions it twice (Rev. 21:23–25 and 22:5). Perhaps John also notices it because Jesus trained him to be aware of light. The subject of light comes up frequently in John's Gospel as well as in his first letter.

In the opening nine verses of the Gospel of John, "light" as a description of Jesus appears six times (1:4–5, 7–9). John tells us that Jesus is the Light.

But all this is introductory. How did John learn about Jesus as light? From Jesus' lips. Early on in His ministry Jesus said, "I am the light of the world. Whoever follows me will not walk in darkness, but will have the light of life" (John 8:12). For other "light" insights in John, see 3:19–21, 9:5, 11:9–10 and 12:35–46.

(continued)

Go Deeper continued

In his first letter, John shows us the importance of recognizing Jesus as the Light even now as we live in a world of darkness. (See 1 John 1:5–7.) In fact we prove each day whether or not we understand the "light," as John points out: "Whoever says he is in the light and hates his brother is still in darkness. Whoever loves his brother abides in the light, and in him there is no cause for stumbling" (1 John 2:9–10).

One of the great sights that can move the heart of a human being is the view of the world from outer space. That blue-green globe spinning in the vastness of space is a wonder to behold. But it won't last forever.

The writer of Hebrews quotes Psalm 102 to praise God and make a point about the earth at the same time: "And, 'You, Lord, laid the foundation of the earth in the beginning, and the heavens are the work of your hands; they will perish, but you remain; they will all wear out like a garment, like a robe you will roll them up, like a garment they will be changed. But you are the same, and your years will have no end'" (Heb. 1:10–12).

After millennia of human abuse, the ecological disasters of the tribulation and the 1,000-year reign of Christ, it's not hard to imagine a tired planet, ready for retirement. By then, Paul's observation from Romans 8:18–21 will be undeniably true: "For I consider that the sufferings of this present time are not worth comparing with the glory that is to be revealed to us. For the creation waits with eager longing for the revealing of the sons of God. For the creation was subjected to futility, not willingly, but because of him who subjected it, in hope that the creation itself will be set free from its bondage to decay and obtain the freedom of the glory of the children of God." At the end of Revelation 20, the age of sin ends and the endless age of heaven begins.

As Revelation 21 open, John sees "a new heaven and a new earth" (v. 1). The world doesn't get cleaned up; it gets transformed into a new, improved model, suited for eternal living. Before he can describe much about the new earth, John sees the "new Jerusalem, coming down out of heaven from God" (v. 2).

" We're so used to thinking of heaven as something 'up there' that it catches us by surprise to discover that heaven will actually come down to the new here. We've talked about going to be with God, yet the age of heaven begins with God coming to dwell with us. "

As the city descends, a voice announces, "Behold, the dwelling place of God is with man. He will dwell with them, and they will be his people, and God himself will be with them as their God" (v. 3). We're so used to thinking of heaven as something "up there" that it catches us by surprise to discover that heaven will actually come down to the new here. We've talked about going to be with God, yet the age of heaven begins with God coming to dwell with us.

What started with Jesus' visit to earth in order to provide salvation and continued with the Holy Spirit's arrival as our indwelling Comforter will now culminate in God the Father's arrival as a permanent resident with us. And He brings, as an earth-warming gift, a residence (a city) for all of us to share.

One of the striking features that make the New Jerusalem a city like no other is that it appears to be the bridge between the new heaven and the new earth. Because we're not accustomed to the measurements John mentions, we might not at first grasp the shear magnitude of the holy city. Translated into modern terms, the New Jerusalem would cover about two-thirds of the United States. John tells us the city is approximately 1,500 miles wide, 1,500 miles long and 1,500 miles high. Talk about skyscrapers!

As we try to imagine the scope of this city, we might pause to remember Jesus' great promise, "In my Father's house are many rooms. If it were not so, would I have told you that I go to prepare a place for you? And if I go and prepare a place for you, I will come again and will take you to myself, that where I am you may be also" (John 14:2–3). Does one of those "rooms" have your name on the door?

Although his task is impossible, John tries to convey some of the amazing landmarks of the city. The city is four-sided and each side has three gates, to make a total of 12. Each of the gates bears the name of one of Israel's original tribes. The city's foundation bears the names of the original apostles. What we think of as prized possessions to be horded and guarded are used as common building materials in the New Jerusalem.

Even today, the skylines of many cities are still recognizable by the particular church steeples that overshadow the rest of the buildings. But John tells us there's no temple in New Jerusalem. God lives in the city. His presence makes no special building necessary. How often do we recognize this is true even today? Church buildings may be convenient and useful for meeting purposes, but they are not essential to the life of the Body of Christ. And often buildings can even limit and divide believers. But life in New Jerusalem, with God's direct presence, will be a wonderful place to spend eternity. Make sure you're there!

Express It

Read John 14:1–6 as you prepare to pray. Talk to God about the immediate implications of Jesus' promise (Is your heart troubled in any way?) and about the future implications of Jesus' promise (How do you feel about having a place reserved in the Father's house?). Meditate in His presence about your response to Jesus' challenge, "Believe also in me."

Consider It

As you read Revelation 21:1–27, consider these questions:

1) How does the description of New Jerusalem compare with the scenes you have imagined about heaven?

_____

_____

_____

2) What promises did John hear God make as New Jerusalem came down (vv. 5–7)?

_____

_____

_____

3) How does New Jerusalem represent her Architect and Builder?

_____

_____

_____

4) What will be the source of light for New Jerusalem?

_____

_____

_____

5) What will be absent in New Jerusalem?

_____

_____

_____

6) In what ways are you looking forward to dwelling in New Jerusalem?

_____

_____

_____

7) Whom or what do you want to see first? Why?

_____

_____

_____

Lesson 13

Eternal Living

It's easy to get caught up in the day-to-day grind of life. But in this lesson, John gives you a look at a time when life will no longer be a chore. Every moment will be a celebration of life. Passages like this have brought hope to many people in their darkest hours; let it be a light to you too.

Revelation 22:1–7

The River of Life

22Then the angel showed me the river of the water of life, bright as crystal, flowing from the throne of God and of the Lamb ²through the middle of the street of the city; also, on either side of the river, the tree of life with its twelve kinds of fruit, yielding its fruit each month. The leaves of the tree were for the healing of the nations. ³No longer will there be anything accursed, but the throne of God and of the Lamb will be in it, and his servants will worship him. ⁴They will see his face, and his name will be on their foreheads. ⁵And night will be no more. They will need no light of lamp or sun, for the Lord God will be their light, and they will reign forever and ever.

Jesus Is Coming

⁶And he said to me, "These words are trustworthy and true. And the Lord, the God of the spirits of the prophets, has sent his angel to show his servants what must soon take place."

⁷"And behold, I am coming soon. Blessed is the one who keeps the words of the prophecy of this book."

> # Key Verse
>
> *No longer will there be anything accursed, but the throne of God and of the Lamb will be in it, and his servants will worship him* (Rev. 22:3).

Go Deeper

Jesus told John, "I am coming soon" (Rev. 22:7). Reading that promise after almost 2,000 years does raise the question of what Jesus meant by "soon." Some have tried to explain all that Revelation teaches as something that has already taken place, past events during John's lifetime.

Since we have not taken that approach here, let's think about what "soon" may mean. First, we must never use "soon" as a basis for waiting by thinking "soon" isn't "now," so I can put off considering Christ awhile longer.

Second, Jesus made it clear that every generation of His followers were to live in full expectation that He could return any day.

(continued)

Go Deeper Continued

(See Matt. 24:36–51.) This explains, in part, why Christians have always been able to equate events around them with biblical prophecy and reasonably expect that Jesus could come. We simply believe today that the signs are clearer than they have been since Jesus' promise to return.

P eople have always preferred to live near water. Cities cluster near rivers. Water is life. We can't survive without it. It's almost as if hidden among our inner desires lies a sense that we were meant to live eternally by a river.

Just as our physical life is sustained by water, so our eternal life will be sustained by the river of life. As John continues his description of New Jerusalem in chapter 22, he describes this river of life that springs from God's throne and runs through the city. Could it be that the only direct contact between the great city and the earth is a breathtaking waterfall of the river of life cascading from one of the walls? What a glorious sight!

The banks of the river of life are lined with a colonnade of specimens of the tree of life. It produces a different kind of fruit each month, and like the aloe vera plant, the leaves of the tree of life have a special medicinal potency. In some way the leaves promote "the healing of the nations" (v. 2). When we look at the world today, we observe that people sometimes make peace much quicker than the nations from which they come. There's little indication that nations will be eternal. People live forever, not nations.

In the kingdom of God all the friction, hatred, and separateness that has traditionally given nations their reasons to exist will no longer apply. Revelation 21:27 points out that "nothing unclean will ever enter" the city. Revelation 22:3 adds that "no longer will there be anything accursed" within the city. The diversity of peoples from every nation, tribe and tongue will be a variety of beauty, not division.

At the headwaters of the river of life, the throne of God will draw all people. It will not be a place of politics or business, but a place of

Third, none of us have to wait longer than a lifetime to see Jesus. And none of us knows how long our life will be. But it seems biblically reasonable to say that the next thing we will be conscious of after we die is the coming of Christ. (See 1 Thess. 4:13–18.) In that sense, meeting Jesus "soon" does take on a sense of urgency. The question is, how much does the possibility of Jesus coming today affect the way you live?

worship. The sound of bubbling, living water in God's presence is sure to bring about a sense of well-being and wholeness to all. In God's throne room we will all be reminded of the life-giving words of Jesus to a lonely, hurting woman by Jacob's well in Samaria: "Everyone who drinks of this water will be thirsty again, but whoever drinks of the water that I will give him will never be thirsty forever. The water that I will give him will become in him a spring of water welling up to eternal life" (John 4:13–14). We will feel most at home before God's throne in the eternal city.

New Jerusalem will be a city of light. The rhythm of life in eternity will be different. We're used to the cycle of day and night because God designed our physical bodies with the capacity to rest and rebuild while sleeping at night. Our eternal bodies will not need rest in the same way we've needed it here.

Curiously, the Bible sometimes speaks of heaven as entering rest. (See Heb. 4:1–10.) It will be a place where we never get tired of anything we do. We will forget all the different kinds of tired we experience here: boredom, exhaustion, depression, and old age. We will live in true light, the light of God's presence. It is truly a life we can now only "see in a mirror dimly, but then face to face" (1 Cor. 13:12).

We can't handle that light now. But then we will thoroughly enjoy it. It will be a light that not only allows us to see objects; but also allows us to know one another in ways we cannot on this side of eternity. The apostle Paul concluded the remark above by saying, "Now I know in part; then I shall know fully, even as I have been fully known" (1 Cor. 13:12). In heaven, we'll see everything much more clearly!

The last two verses in this passage bring us back to a theme from the beginning of Revelation. In 1:3 we were promised a blessing if

> " *Whether or not 'soon' means today, will we be faithful today to 'keep' what we've learned from God's Word?* "

we read, hear, and keep "what is written" in this book. Here (22:7), the blessing is simply repeated by stating the last step: "And behold, I am coming soon. Blessed is the one who keeps the words of the prophecy of this book." Both these verses convey a strong tone of urgency with the phrase "what must soon take place" (v. 6) and "I am coming soon."

When we read a prophetic passage like this it's easy to get caught up in figuring out what will happen *next* and miss the importance of what needs to happen *now*. Urgent application for us is this: whether or not "soon" means today, will we be faithful today to "keep" what we've learned from God's Word?

Express It

Turn your thoughts about that last question into prayer. How has this study of Revelation been a blessing in your life already? Consider the insightful moments during this study when you've gotten a fresh glimpse of the glorified Christ. Think along with the hymn writer who expressed the wonder of looking fully into Christ's face and discovering that the things of earth "grow strangely dim in the light of His glory and grace" (from Helen Lemmel's hymn, "Turn Your Eyes Upon Jesus"). Speak to God about how you envision that experience.

Consider It

As you read Revelation 22:1–7, consider these questions:

1) Between this section and 21:8–27, what will not be seen or experienced in the New Jerusalem?

_____

_____

_____

_____

2) Describe the relationship God will have with His people in the eternal city?

_____

_____

_____

_____

3) Based on these seven verses, what observations can you make about God's character?

_____

_____

_____

_____

4) How do you respond when you read a passage like this that promises Jesus' imminent arrival (see **Go Deeper**)?

_____

_____

_____

_____

5) How has this study of Revelation been a blessing in your life already?

_____

_____

_____

_____

Between Now and Then

While the time of Jesus' return is still to come, in this lesson you'll be reminded how to live each day in the here and now. Though we don't know when Jesus will come back, we are to live in eager expectation of His return. The promises and blessings of Revelation are for the ones who hear it and then let it affect their lives.

Revelation 22:8–21

[8]I, John, am the one who heard and saw these things. And when I heard and saw them, I fell down to worship at the feet of the angel who showed them to me, [9]but he said to me, "You must not do that! I am a fellow servant with you and your brothers the prophets, and with those who keep the words of this book. Worship God."

[10]And he said to me, "Do not seal up the words of the prophecy of this book, for the time is near. [11]Let the evildoer still do evil, and the filthy still be filthy, and the righteous still do right, and the holy still be holy."

[12]"Behold, I am coming soon, bringing my recompense with me, to repay everyone for what he has done. [13]I am the Alpha and the Omega, the first and the last, the beginning and the end."

[14]Blessed are those who wash their robes, so that they may have the right to the tree of life and that they may enter the city by the gates. [15]Outside are the dogs and sorcerers and the sexually immoral and murderers and idolaters, and everyone who loves and practices falsehood.

[16]"I, Jesus, have sent my angel to testify to you about these things for the churches. I am the root and the descendant of David, the bright morning star."

[17]The Spirit and the Bride say, "Come." And let the one who hears say, "Come." And let the one who is thirsty come; let the one who desires take the water of life without price.

[18]I warn everyone who hears the words of the prophecy of this book: if anyone adds to them, God will add to him the plagues described in this book, [19]and if anyone takes away from the words of the book of this prophecy, God will take away his share in the tree of life and in the holy city, which are described in this book.

[20]He who testifies to these things says, "Surely I am coming soon." Amen. Come, Lord Jesus!

[21]The grace of the Lord Jesus be with all. Amen.

Key Verse

"Behold, I am coming soon, bringing my recompense with me, to repay everyone for what he has done" (Rev. 22:12).

Go Deeper

There are two blessings promised in chapter 22. There are seven in all offered throughout the Book of Revelation (1:3; 14:13; 16:15; 19:9; 20:6; and 22:7,14). In a book full of sevens, in which seven has a particular connection with God's actions, these references to blessing cannot be accidental. The term for blessing is identical to the one Jesus used when he began the Sermon on the Mount. In fact, we could call these the Beatitudes of Revelation. The God who judges is the very same God who blesses.

Take a few moments and read through each of the references to blessing in Revelation. Note that all of them can be applied to you, now. Three of them have to do with consequences of actions you take:

A ngels have always been awe-inspiring. When angelic messengers appeared to humans, they invariably had to assure us to "fear not." At some point in the experience of receiving the vision that became the Book of Revelation, John became conscious that he was keeping company with an angel. The thought overwhelmed him.

As he put it, "I fell down to worship at the feet of the angel who showed them to me" (Rev. 22:8). For once, it was an angel's turn to be amazed. "You must not do that!" (v. 9). In John's time, the worship of angels was a popular form of spirituality. Here, one of the frequent objects of human worship was reminding all of us that who we worship is as important as worship itself. Today we see a fascination with "spirituality" of every kind. The angel would say the same thing to people today that he said to John: "Worship God." No thing and no one else is worthy of that kind of attention from us.

When John was instructed not to "seal up the words of the prophecy of this book" (v. 10), the meaning is apparent. God did not reveal His plans to have them hidden but heeded. These are warnings and invitations to be acted on by people in any age, including the years of tribulation. Those who pay attention to Revelation will be blessed.

Beginning at verse 12, Jesus speaks again. He renews His promise to come soon, bringing both reward and judgment. His titles as Alpha, Omega, first, last, the beginning and end, describe His eternal

1) You have to be in the Lord in order to die in the Lord (14:13); 2) You have to belong to the Lamb in order to receive the invitation to the Lamb's supper (19:9); and 3) You must be dead in Christ to share in the first resurrection.

The other four references to blessing indicate results from the way you live and respond to God's Word today: 1) You can read, hear and keep His Word today; 2) You can "stay awake" (16:15) and be alert to God's moving in your life; 3) You can focus on keeping His Word, applying it in your life (22:7); and 4) You can "wash your robe," living under the continual cleansing of God's grace, remembering, "If we confess our sins, he is faithful and just to forgive us our sins and to cleanse us from all unrighteousness" (1 John 1:9). I urge you to live a life in God's continual blessing.

role. They point to what Paul describes in Colossians 1:16: "For by him all things were created, in heaven and on earth, visible and invisible, whether thrones or dominions or rulers or authorities—all things were created through him and for him." He has the right as our Creator to hold us accountable for our obedience. Those who don't obey will remain outside of the eternal city and be confined to the lake of fire. (See Rev. 20:11–15, 22:15.)

Revelation 22:16 represents the first time since the last word in chapter 3 that the Church of Jesus Christ is mentioned. Yet these things have been revealed "for the churches." All the future participants look back from the vantage point of prophecy and invite, "Come" (v. 17). The Book of Revelation reveals Jesus Christ as one who invites and saves. Those who reject the invitation to forgiveness and eternal life have no one to blame but themselves. Jesus offers "the water of life without price" (v. 17)—He offers it freely.

The last four verses of Revelation are a sobering contrast to the offer of blessing for those who read and heed the book. Anyone who "adds" to them (who requires his or her book or study guide in addition to the Bible) or "takes away from the words of the book of this prophecy" (who claims these are only the words of humans or mere myths) will receive an appropriate punishment. Disregard for the message of this book will not be highly regarded by the God who knows and controls the future. The book ends with the third promise by Jesus in this chapter, "I am coming soon" (v. 20). This last time,

> *" The constantly amazing discovery in the Christian life is that the Lord Jesus not only takes up residence in us, but also works through us to bring glory to His name. "*

the Lord adds "surely" to the statement, making it emphatic. To which John provides the most appropriate answer we could possibly give: "Amen. Come, Lord Jesus!"

Our study of Revelation brings us to that decision which faces us every day in following Jesus Christ. We know He is coming for us or we are going to Him. We don't know the day or the hour, but we know He has laid out each day before us to obey, serve, and enjoy His presence in our lives—for Christ wants to be glorified in us. The constantly amazing discovery in the Christian life is that the Lord Jesus not only takes up residence in us, but also works through us to bring glory to His name. So, for now, we say, "Come, Lord Jesus!" And then we willingly add, "Until You do, Lord, what would You have us do?"

Express It

As you pray, review what you have discovered in this study of Revelation. Thank God for new insights you've received. Be grateful that you have understood more than you expected, and be humble that you haven't understood everything. In the same way we approach the amazing creation of the universe, we approach the re-creation in awe that God allows us to know so much, yet not insisting that we know everything. In the end, we acknowledge that God created, that He will re-create and that He has graciously given us an eternal home with Him. Amen! Come, Lord Jesus.

Consider It

As you read Revelation 22:8–21, consider these questions:

1) How did the overall experience of receiving this vision affect John?

_____

_____

_____

2) In verses 10 and 11, why does the angel insist every one should continue to do what they do—evil, filthiness, righteousness, or holiness?

_____

_____

_____

3) Who does Jesus say is entitled to citizenship in New Jerusalem?

_____

_____

_____

4) What events in your life make it hard to hold out for Christ's return?

_____

_____

_____

_____

5) How do you sense the significance of those who say, "Come" in these verses, and why do they say it?

_____

_____

_____

_____

6) What would you most like to be doing at the moment Jesus returns? Why?

_____

_____

_____

_____

Notes

Notes

Notes

Notes

Notes

Notes

Notes